NUGGETS

Words of Hope and Encouragement

Never Underestimate God's Grace Even Through Suffering

Deb J. Kilgore
Rocks To Nuggets Publishing

813-785-8964

Copyright © 2007 by Deb J. Kilgore

Library of Congress Control Number: 2007928850

ISBN 978-0-9796583-0-3

All rights reserved. No part of this publication may be reproduced, stored in a retrieval system, or transmitted in any form or by any means, electronic, mechanical, photocopying, recording or otherwise, without the prior written permission of the copyright owner.

Cover design: Minuteman Press & Marianne Fisher

Editor: Karen Rumple

For quantity purchases of the book contact:
    Rocks to Nuggets Publishing
    4501 W. Bay to Bay Blvd.
    Tampa, Florida 33629
    (813) 832-1737
    www.rockstonuggets.com

Printed in the United States of America by Minuteman Press.

Romans 15:4

"For everything that was written in the past was written to teach us, so that through endurance and the encouragement of the Scriptures we might have hope." (NIV)

***This book is dedicated
in love & with love
to
my mother***

Jean Jones

Although you were given so little in your life—you have "given" so much to others. What an incredible mother you have been to Linda and Ray, Don and Lisa, and me!

Thank you for your inspiration, support and belief in me during the good and tough times you've seen me go through. You have truly been my best friend.

May you now be blessed with healing, peace and abundant joy!

*Forever & Always,
Your Daughter
Deb*

Introduction

God wants us to be encouraged. He also wants us to encourage others.

One way we can be encouraged and encourage others is through words. I am constantly reminded of how powerful words are. Powerful in a positive way and just as powerful or more powerful in a damaging way. Someone's words can make us feel we are on the top of the mountain and bring feelings of support and affirmation. On the other end of the spectrum, someone's words can discourage, damage and completely destroy our positive thoughts about who we are or our endeavors.

We can always count on **God's Words** to be encouraging. His Words provide a beacon for us as we go forward everyday. In His Word, He promises us that He will see us through. We are reminded over and over that He is our refuge and strength, and in Him we can find Truth.

Many times I have found myself desperately searching for a word, verse or chapter that will calm my heart or even get me through the day or situation. Sometimes I would write the word or verse on a scrap piece of paper and tuck it in my pocket, or write it on the closest thing to me. It would make a difference as I would stop a moment and reflect on what God had put before me.

As years progressed, I had no idea how God was going to expand that concept. His Word became a part of my every day. It was like food or exercise for me. Over time something began to happen. Words began to "pop" off the page and "unfold" to a new dimension. It was insight and understanding of words, taking them to a different level. I had to start writing them down because I found I couldn't remember them a short time later. It was strange to me— I always had a great memory especially when I created an idea or concept. I was an educator for 15 years and it was an expectation to recall information. This was strangely different!

It was as if I was just the recorder.

Over the years I have written each word down. I find myself going back to read them when I need strength. I also have shared these "Nuggets" with family, friends, co-workers and complete strangers. They have been written on a handy napkin, index cards, daily calendars, back of an envelope and even in the palm of a hand.

I know they are to be held, used and passed on to others.

So today dear friend, I pass these Nuggets on to you. Hold them close to your heart and absorb the truths they stand on.

Then, take these Nuggets and pass them on to others as it has been purposed. For you and others, blessings will follow.

WHAT'S INSIDE THE NUGGETS...

Dedication   iii
Introduction   v
Acknowledgement   ix

PART I—CAPTURE THESE TO ENRICH YOUR LIFE [8]
Nuggets to hold on to

HOPE	2	MERCY	10
FAITH	4	LOVE	12
GRACE	6	LIGHT	14
PEACE	8	TRUTH	16

PART II—STEPS TO INCREASE YOUR FAITH [23]
Nuggets of action

ACTION	20	FOCUS	44
CRY OUT	22	FOLLOW	46
HELP	24	SERVE	48
BELIEVE	26	SOW	50
APPLY	28	KNOW	52
RELY	30	REAP	54
GRIP	32	VALUE	56
COME	34	OBEY	58
SEEK	36	TRACE	60
TRANSFORM	38	IMAGINE	62
AIM	40	TRUST	64
BUILD	42		

PART III—THESE REQUIRE YOUR IMMEDIATE ATTENTION [11]
Nuggets to be aware of

DOUBT	68	PRIDE	80
FEAR	70	SIN	82
ANGER	72	WAR	84
FOG	74	PAIN	86
SECRETS	76	THE DIRTY D'S	88
ALONE	78		

PART IV–HOLD THESE DEAR TO YOUR HEART [12]
Nuggets to cherish

CORE	92	SOAR	104
SHIELD	94	LET	106
REAL	96	PASSION	108
PRESENCE	98	ARM	110
PROMISE	100	SPIRIT	112
WORD	102	ANGELS	114

PART V–PLAN YOUR WORK, WORK YOUR PLAN [9]
Nuggets to deliver

WILL	118	TAG	128
HIS	120	POP	130
WAIT	122	BOLD	132
FEAR	124	UNITY	134
DEPTH	126		

PART VI–MEDITATE ON THESE PROMISES [11]
Nuggets to notice

ENOUGH	138	VISION	150
AHA	140	RIPE	152
POWER	142	SIGN	154
MORE	144	CALLED	156
PURPOSE	146	SILENCE	158
REVEAL	148		

PART VII–A VALUED GIFT [11]
Nuggets of gold

BLESSED	162	SUDDENLY	174
HEAL	164	JOY	176
WISDOM	166	LAUGH	178
COURAGE	168	AMAZING	180
MIRACLE	170	CELEBRATE	182
FAVOR	172		

Acknowlegdement to the angels in my life:

My mother and father—Roy and Jean Jones
*Thank you for steering me with a focus on faith, perseverance and a
positive outlook on whatever life brings. Your strength and passion
to make the most out of life will forever guide me. I look at what
you both experienced so young in your lives and yet truly trusted that
God can change any circumstance. Thank you for your forever faith
and love that has influenced me in an incredible way.
(Since the writing of this heartfelt dedication, my father has become an
eternal angel. As he dances, golfs, and bowls with the angels above—may he
forever be at peace.)*

My children—Josh, Corrine and Morgan
*Thank you for your belief in me when times were tough for us. You have
brought incredible joy to my life. In you I will always see "Hope."
Thank you for your unending love—it has been all that I needed to press on.
May you always keep your faith in your front pocket—it will see you
through. Josh, always remember Jeremiah 29:11. Corrine, hold on to
Proverbs 2. Morgan, know that Psalm 103—is yours forever.*

My grandsons—Oliver and Sammy and our little angel to come
*To my little bambinos who have inspired me to be the best "Nani" I can
be. Thank you for your "unconditional" love that has reminded me of God's
love and that we all deserve to be loved in this way.*

My mentor and dearest friend—Jan Walther
*Thank you for your encouragement, honest feedback and continual
prayers along the journey. Jan, thank you for many years of support to me
and my children. I know God placed you beside me holding an umbrella,
a shield, and gifts of love that always brought a smile. You have left a deep
footprint on my life.*

My ladybugs, forever friends—Julie McGinley, Jackie McPherson, and Trish Anton
*Jewels—your belief in me has been surmountable! Thank you for always
listening and giving good sound advice when needed. Jackie—I love our
long distance coffee meetings. You are a perfect example of how God wants
us to suit up and show up. It has been so encouraging to walk this path
together. Trish—your spirit of enthusiasm is contagious and your support
is priceless. Isn't it amazing how 2 Minnesotans ended up in Florida at the
same time?*

My dear friend–Marianne Fisher

I am so grateful that you are who you are. Thank you for not only listening to the "Spirit" but acting on it. I will never forget you telling me what needed to be done to get this book to completion. I thought you were crazy at first. The timing was not at all what I thought was possible... so, it is evident that He used you to get me back to writing. Thank you for being so tuned in that you heard the task at hand. You are such a special person in my life and have come to mean so much to me.

My miracle friend–Carla Wiza

Through a lot of pain we were brought together. Thank you for reaching out for truth, overcoming the odds and at the same time helping me make my dream come true.

A special thank you to my dear editor, Karen Rumple, for her endless devotion to edit Nuggets, and Ken Timmons for the development of my website. You are both incredible examples of servants of God offering your gifts to this purpose.

In closing... I want each of my family and all my friends to know my appreciation of your words of encouragement, support and love that has been instrumental in the journey of Nuggets.

Jeremiah 36:17-18

"And they asked Baruch saying, 'Tell us now, how did you write all these words—at His instruction?' So Baruch answered them. 'He proclaimed with His mouth all these words to me, and I wrote them with ink in the book.'" (NKJV)

God told Jeremiah to write.

        Jeremiah told Baruch to write.

                Baruch wrote for all to read.

PART I

CAPTURE THESE TO ENRICH YOUR LIFE

Nuggets to hold on to

"We need never shout across the spaces to an absent God. He is nearer than our own soul, closer than own soul, closer than our most secret thoughts."

A.W. Tozer

HOPE

Hold
Onto
Promises
Everyday

"If it were not for hope–
the heart would break."

John Ray (1628-1705)

Romans 4:18-20
"Against all hope, Abraham in hope believed and so believed and so became the Father of many nations...Yet he did not waver through unbelief regarding the promise of God, but was strengthened in his faith and gave glory to God, being fully persuaded that God had power to do what He had promised." (NIV)

Almost 9 years ago the word "Hope" came to me during a time that I was feeling quite "Hopeless." In fact, I was truly ready to "throw in the towel" as they say. Everything was caving in around me. I felt betrayed, lonely and quite desperate.

As I closed my eyes in the shower, crying from the pit of my stomach, I prayed that God would help me. I cried out. In that dark moment, I actually saw the word HOPE with just the instruction I needed.

Hold
Onto
Promises
Everyday

{As I saw this word, I questioned it, as nothing like this had ever happened to me before. I felt God was saying, "I will hold you Deb, put your hope in Me."}

Immediately after God showed me this sign of HOPE, my 3 children began knocking on the bathroom door. They needed me! They depended on me at that time of their lives. How could I even think of giving up? Interesting... as hopeless as I felt, I was their hope. From that point on, hope had a new meaning to me.

God would see us through. It's His promise. He will see you through also.

Your thoughts…

FAITH

Find
Answers
In
The
Hope

*"Faith leads us beyond ourselves–
It leads us directly to God."*

*Pope John Paul II
(1920-2005)*

Hebrews 11:1
"Now faith is being sure of what we hope for and certain of what we do not see." (NIV)

In one of the study guides I use frequently, I read the following on faith. Faith…is a choice rather than an ability. We can always choose to believe or to commit to His Word regardless of the magnitude of the challenge. (NKJV-Study Guide)

It hasn't been easy walking forward in faith. But when I realized it was a choice for me and I could ask God to help me, I didn't feel so overwhelmed. Each time I saw an answered prayer I knew that hope and faith went hand in hand.

Faith is looking at God not the mountain, and never giving up.

I love the quote by Stanley Baldwin who wrote…
"I am one of those who would rather sink with faith than swim without it."

What is your hope right now? How is your faith around that hope? Choose to increase your faith by praying and speaking out your confidence in God to fulfill your hope.

Your thoughts…

GRACE

Giving up & Growing
Receiving
All
Christ's
Energies

"Grace is the tangible expression of God's love for each of us."

Leith Anderson

2 Corinthians 12:9a
"And He said to me, My grace is sufficient for you, for my strength is made perfect in weakness."(NKJV)

Grace is the central invitation to life and the final word. It is the beckoning nudge and the overwhelming, undeserved mercy which nudges and urges us to change and grow–and then gives us the power to pull it off.

God loves us so much that he gives us the gift of grace. Grace is when we know that we are being treated better than we deserve–it is unmerited favor of God. It's unexplainable and remarkable. Practice speaking grace into each mountain you face. Expect great power and great grace to bring about the essence of God.

It's essence is free flowing…Grace.

Your thoughts…

PEACE

Pain
Erased
And
Calmness
Evolves

"Nothing real can be threatened. Nothing unreal exists. Herein lies the peace of God."

The Course of Miracles

John 14:27
"Peace I leave with you; my peace I give you. I do not give it to you as the world gives. Do not let your hearts be troubled and do not be afraid." (NIV)

Peace comes from the Greek word ***shalom***, meaning wholeness or completeness. This word occurs 250 times in the Old Testament. Through the life of Christ we can experience this wholeness or peace. Nothing is more fulfilling to me than to feel God's peace in my life. Things can be falling down all around me, but the inner peace God gives me, allows me to walk calmly and forward with great confidence.

My prayer for you today is that you will feel God's peace today in an incredible way.

Your thoughts…

MERCY

Meeting
Everyone
Right where
Christ sees
You

"It is not how much we do, but how much we put into the doing."

Mother Teresa

Proverbs 11:17
"The merciful man does good to his own soul." (NKJV)

Micah 6:8
"He has shown you, O man, what is good, and what does the Lord require of you? To do justly, to love mercy and to walk humbly with your God?" (NIV)

My dear friend, Jan, comes to mind for many people when thinking of a person who lives a merciful life. For 11 years I have observed and witnessed her loving kindness to people like no other. After a full week, year after year, of serving as a Junior High School Counselor–she spent almost every Saturday buzzing around a list of Seniors' shopping, helping and visiting, always providing a service of meeting their needs. As a retiree she continues to serve with a merciful heart daily.

Jan has and continues to exemplify a selfless life of mercy for others.

Do you have a merciful heart toward others? How can you show mercy to someone today by seeing them like Christ sees them?

Your thoughts…

LOVE

Love
Others
Vitally
Everyday

"There is more hunger for love and appreciation in this world than for bread."

Mother Teresa

John 4:11
"Beloved if God so loved us, we also ought to love one another. My command is this; Love each other as I have loved you." (NIV)

It feels so good when we can give love to others. I feel it is a way we can demonstrate the kind of love God has for each of us. As I have grown in my faith over the years, I've come to believe in the need and strength of first understanding how much God loves us just as we are. As we realize how much we are loved, we are able to love others freely, asking for nothing in return.

When we love unconditionally as God loves us…something begins to happen. Something good **EVOL**VES out of His love.

It all begins with **L-O-V-E**. No matter how you look at it. It is there.

L
O
V
E
———
E
V
O
L
———
V
E
S

Your thoughts…

LIGHT

Living
In
God's
House of
Truth

"There are two ways of spreading light: To be the candle or the mirror that reflects it."

Edith Wharton

John 3:21
"But whoever lives by the truth comes into the light, so that it may be seen plainly that what he has done has been done through God." (NIV)

My youngest daughter, Morgan, and I were at a restaurant when she brought to my attention the dynamic skyline. There was a significant line of dark clouds across the sky with no light at all. Beneath this equally was a significant line of white clouds as if the light was directly behind them wanting to burst through. It was a sight I had never seen before. Morgan remarked that it looked like a representation of heaven and hell, truth and darkness. It was amazing as we watched a split occur and light began to seep through the line that separated the two.

At the same time, directly above in the darkness of the clouds, an opening appeared and an incredible burst of light broke through.

In a matter of minutes a transformation occurred. The light changed the entire view. Morgan and I continued to sit and let the light shine directly on us. A couple sitting by us got up and moved due to the brightness. We remained soaking up the light, mesmerized by the transformation.

As God's Word tells us in Isaiah 60 and Debby Boone summarizes, "Exposing ourselves to the light and presence of the Lord's love not only will uncover the dark places of our heart, but also will fill them with light so that the glory of the Lord rises upon you."

Soak it up.

Your thoughts…

TRUTH

To
Recognize &
Understand
Total
Honesty

"Truth is the only safe ground to stand upon."

Elizabeth Cady Stanton

Psalm 25:4-5
"Show me Your ways, O Lord; Teach me Your paths. Lead me in Your truth and teach me, for You are the God of my salvation; On You I wait all the day." (NKJV)

Today at our service a woman…the woman at the well… came to remind us of the truth Jesus stands on. At that well, the place she had been to many times, she found truth that would change her life like never before. The truth of Jesus.

As I watched her in complete simplicity—no makeup and dressed in cloaks of that time—she met Jesus completely as she truly was. Ready to face the truth.

Can you visualize yourself at the well face to face with Jesus? Just as you are? Know that He will guide you and direct you in truth. You will be set free. Standing on truth and only truth will lead you in ways that will glorify Him.

Your thoughts…

PART II

STEPS TO INCREASE YOUR FAITH

Nuggets of action

"To keep a lamp burning, we have to keep putting oil in it."

Mother Teresa

ACTION

Acknowledge He is God
Call upon Him
Take to heart His words
Increase Your Faith
Obey His commands
Need Him

"In our era, the road to holiness necessarily passes through the world of action."

Unknown

Psalm 105:1-2
"Oh, give thanks to the Lord. Call upon His Name. Make known His deeds among the peoples! Sing to Him, sing psalms to Him; Talk of all His wondrous works!" (NKJV)

God is a God of action. He expects us to be servants of action. Otherwise nothing would change. In Psalm 105, the first 5 verses have 8 verbs telling us exactly what we should do. It instructs us to be an "Action Figure" for Christ.

We are to **give, call, make, sing, talk, rejoice, seek and remember.**

What is the action in your faith?
Do you **acknowledge** God in your life?
Do you **call** upon Him? Do you **believe**?

Be an "Action Figure" for the Father.
Act upon His Word.

Your thoughts…

CRY OUT

"At fifteen life had taught me undeniably that surrender, in its place, was as honorable as resistance, especially if one had no choice."

Maya Angelou

Call to Me (Jeremiah 33:3)
Rely on Me (1 Chronicles 16:10-11)
Yearn for Me to help you (Psalm 61)

Psalm 61:1-4
"Hear my cry, O God;
Listen to my prayer.
From the ends of the earth
I call to you,
I call as my heart grows faint;
Lead me to the rock that is higher than I.
For you have been my refuge
A strong tower against the foe,
I long to dwell in your tent forever
And take refuge in the shelter of your wings." (NIV)

When we get to a point of crying out we can surrender. Surrendering allows God to show us His love for us. We rely on Him instead of ourselves. This is when we need and want to climb under the shelter of His wings. Visualize our mighty God with his wings around you as you are curled up under His presence.

We allow Him to help us. The more we allow Him to help, the more we are able to receive from Him.

What circumstance are you in or do you have on you that He can hold and you can receive His help?

Your thoughts…

HELP

"I don't know who–or what–put the question, I don't know when it was put, I don't even remember answering. But at some moment I did answer yes to someone–or something–and from that hour I was certain that existence is meaningful and that, therefore, my life, in self-surrender, had a goal."

Dag Hammarskjold

Hold me, Lord
Encourage me, Lord
Lift me up, Lord
Promise you will never leave me, Lord!

Psalm 37:40
"And the Lord shall help them and deliver them. He shall deliver them from the wicked and save them because they trust in Him."(NKJV)

How are you when it comes to asking for help? I have to be one of the most stubborn people when it comes to reaching out for assistance. Deep inside I think it represents weakness. Although I don't want to think that way, I know it has been an issue for me.

The last 11 years I have asked for help in more ways than I have ever thought. I have been in a position that I have had to let go of my pride and let God and others help me. He is our greatest source of help as He is the "Helper of the fatherless." (Psalm 10:14)

Do you need help in any areas? First, let go and let God Help you. He will send you all the help you can receive.

Your thoughts...

BELIEVE

Bold
Example to
Live with Christ's
Internal peace and
Expectation,
Valuing forever–
Eternal peace

*"I believe in the sun even when it is not shining,
I believe in love even when not feeling it,
I believe in God even when He is silent."*

Unknown–Wall inscription in a cellar hideout during the Holocaust

2 Chronicles 20:20
"Believe in the Lord your God, and you shall be established; believe His prophets, and you shall prosper." (NKJV)

What does it mean to truly believe?
Strong's concordance of the word, ***believe*** #539, is stated;
To be firm, stable, established; also, to be firmly persuaded; **to believe– solidly**. In its causative form *aman* means "to believe" that is, to **"consider trustworthy."**

This is the word used in Genesis 15:6 when Abraham "believed" in the Lord. In the verse above in Chronicles, *aman* appears two times in one verse and could be translated: "Be established in the Lord… and you will be established." From *aman* comes *emunah*–faith. The most famous derivative is *amen*, which conveys this idea: It is solidly, firmly, surely true, verified and established.

When I first came upon this verse in Chronicles 20:20, the first thing that came to my mind was perfect vision. I wondered if I could creatively make a correlation. As I began studying the concordance in my Bible it was coined perfectly, a great affirmation.

Develop spiritual 20/20 vision: Choose to believe the Bible as the absolute Word of God. Rely upon its witness to God's nature, character and promises. Believe the words of those who proclaim God's Word.

I choose to believe. I want to believe in a way that it is evident to others in the way I choose to live. That it is not only what I say, but more importantly, the way I live day by day. Not doubting, but living in a confident knowing, that **God is established in me.**

Your thoughts…

APPLY

Ask for His
Power &
Presence to
Live in
You

"At that moment I experienced the presence of the Divine as I had never before experienced Him. It seemed as though I could hear the quiet assurance of an inner voice saying, 'Stand up for righteousness, stand up for truth. God will be at your side forever.'
Almost at once my fears began to pass from me. My uncertainty disappeared. I was ready to face anything. The outer situation remained the same, but God had given me inner calm."

Martin Luther King, Jr.
(1929-1968)

Psalm 90:17
"And let the beauty of the Lord our God be upon us, and establish the work of our hands for us." (NKJV)

For many years I had a faith that I kept in control. It always looked great on the outside. I looked like Super Mom, Wife, Teacher, Church Leader and "Susie on the spot" for community leadership. As a man or woman, have you dealt with the need to be in control of your life?

I applied myself alright...I did it all! As I look back–it was covering many painful empty spots in my marriage, in my life.

But through the honesty and innocence of my own 3 children and of the precious children I was blessed to teach, I began to acknowledge what I was missing in my own life. I wanted complete truth in my life. I wanted simplicity, peace and laughter. When I ran out of steam and could no longer do it anymore–I let God take over. I realized that if I applied my trust in Him–He would give me the strength, peace, grace and power to do what I needed to do. He also helped me deal with the painful spots, too.

Apply your faith. Seek Him like never before. Believe in His promises. Count on Him to come through for you.
Your thoughts…

RELY

"If we really belong to God then we must be at His disposal and we must never be preoccupied with the future. There is no reason to be.

God is there."

Mother Teresa

Recognize God is always faithful
Exercise your faith
Live with expectations
Yearn for His will to be done first

Psalm 37:3-4
"Trust in the Lord, and do good; Dwell in the land, and feed on His faithfulness. Delight yourself also in the Lord. And He shall give you the desires of your heart." (NKJV)

As I was visiting a church a couple years ago, the pastor asked 6 men to come in front of the church. The pastor was standing above them as the podium was elevated 6-8 feet. His request to the 6 volunteers was for them to catch him. They quickly arranged their positions to do so. The pastor, a sizable gentleman which created nervousness in the congregation, removed his glasses in preparing to jump. Right as we were anticipating his leap–we gasped–he stopped.

He wanted to illustrate what believing and trusting were all about.

We rely on God when we believe and actively trust. Relying on Him requires active action.

Are you relying on God in all areas of your life? Rely and expect remarkable results.

Your thoughts…

GRIP

Graciously
Receive God's
Intense
Plan and Purpose

"A man should conceive of a legitimate purpose in his heart, and set out to accomplish it. He should make this purpose the centralizing point of his thoughts. It may take the form of a spiritual ideal, or it may be a worldly object, according to his nature at the time being; but whichever it is, he should steadily focus his thought forces upon the object which he has set before him. He should make this purpose his supreme duty, and should devote himself to its attainment, not allowing his thoughts to wander away into ephemeral fancies, longings, and imaginings. This is the royal road to self-control and true concentration of thought. Even if he fails again and again to accomplish his purpose (as he necessarily must until weakness is overcome), the strength of character gained will be the measure of his true success, and this will form a new starting point for future power and triumph. "

Unknown

Psalm 32:8
"I will instruct you and teach you in the way you should go; I will guide you with my eye." (NKJV)

When one of my mentors told me she thought I should read about Hannah, I took her instruction. She expressed that she kept seeing my name when she was studying Hannah's life.

I learned that Hannah was focused. Her HOPE gave her an intense dream that gripped her life. I became so excited knowing that I could, with God's help, be more like Hannah. I asked God right then and there to GRIP my life.

How about you? Take God's grip and let Him pull you up no matter where you are right now. He will allow you to hold on to one finger or His entire hand…whatever you need. Basically, whatever you allow Him to do.

As He grips you—He will show you what to do next, how to handle your situation, and give you all you need to live out His plan and purpose for your life.

Your thoughts…

COME

Count
On
Me in
Every way

"God promises to keep us in the palm of His hand, with or without awareness. God has already made a space for us, even if we have not made a space for God."

David & Barbara Sorenson

Matthew 11:28
"Come unto me all you who are weary and burdened and I will give you rest." (NIV)

Matthew 4:19
"'Come follow me,' Jesus said, 'and I will make you fishers of men.' At once they left the boat and their father and followed Him." (NIV)

Picture this…

Our Heavenly Father sitting calmly and peaceful with both arms extended out with His palms slightly turned toward us. And here we all are running around trying to **be** more, **have** more, **do** more. As we become engulfed in this world, our Father stays constant. If we could just stop a moment, what would we see, what would we hear?

Imagine God looking at you directly and with his voice and the movement of his hand echoes the word…

"Come"

Today I come.

Your thoughts…

SEEK

Search &
Examine
Eternal
Knowledge

"Only as high as I reach can I grow, only as far as I seek can I go, only as deep as I look can I see, only as much as I dream can I be."

Karen Raven

Matthew 6:33
"But seek first the kingdom of God and His righteousness, and all these things shall be added unto you." (NKJV)

As I was listening to a song at our church it came to me clearly… I want to be a seeker. The words of the song were:

Lord, we want to know you
Live our lives to show you
Lord we want to know you
We are seekers of your heart..

What does it mean to seek? According to the Strong #1245 explanation, seek derives from the word ***bagash (bah-kahsh)***. To seek is to diligently look for, to search earnestly until the object of the search is located. ***Bagash*** occurs more than 210 times in the Bible. We are to search for the Lord's face; His presence, must especially be sought.

What are you seeking for in your life? How would your friends and family answer that question about you? Are you a seeker of God's heart? What do you spend time looking for and working toward?

Your thoughts…

TRANSFORM

To
Radically change
Accepting a
New
Spirit
From
Our
Restorer, Our
Maker

"It is an invitation to our souls, a mysterious voice reverberating within, a tug on our hearts that can neither be ignored nor denied. It contains, by definition, the purest message and promise of essential freedom. It touches us at the center of our awareness. When such a call occurs and we hear it—really hear it—our shift to higher consciousness is assured. As the twelfth-century rabbinical authority, physician and philosopher said, 'The sound of the shofar calls to us: Awaken sleepers, from your sleep, arise; slumberers, from your slumber, and examine your deeds..... Look after your own souls, and improve your ways.'"

Unknown

Romans 12:2
"Do not be conformed to this world, but be transformed by the renewing of your mind, that you may prove what *is* that good and acceptable and perfect will of God." (NKJV)

Paul gives us instruction in this verse to not be conformed, either inwardly or in appearance, to the values, ideas, and behavior of a fallen world.

Instead, we are to be transformed. The definition of **transform** is to change radically in inner character, condition or nature.

How does this happen for us? We should continually renew our minds through prayer and by studying God's Word. By the power of the Holy Spirit you will be transformed and made like the image of Christ.

Pray for transformation from the inside out. Let His power and presence work within you.

Your thoughts…

AIM

Abide
In
Me

"Act like you expect to get into the end zone."

Joe Paterno

John 8:31-32
"Then Jesus said to those Jews who believed Him, 'If you abide in my word you are my disciples indeed. And you shall know the truth and the truth shall make you free.'" (NKJV)

With God in our life–there is always room for more. More signs of Him, more peace, more miracles, more joy.

We had just made the move to Florida. As I was driving my daughter to school, I kept thinking about my writing and completion of this book. For several years, I felt that God was whispering, "You'll finish your book by the water front." In the 1st week of being here–I felt strong that I needed to commit my early morning time to Him. As I dropped my daughter off at school, I turned the radio up. Immediately the verse of the day was shared, John 8:31-32.

The speaker stressed the importance of us abiding in God's Word. I realized that through this move, all the unpacking and trying to transition, I had not been in God's Word in a week or more. At that moment I committed to spend my morning time to allow God to finish His writings. Suddenly, the word "AIM" was revealed. **Abide in Me**.

Aim for the light of God to shine in you. He will show you more. Aim high my friend–with Him there are no limits.

Your thoughts…

BUILD

> *"I think what we are longing for is not "the good life" as it's been advertised to us in the American dream, but life in its fullness, its richness, its abundance. Living more reflectively helps us enter into that fullness."*
>
> *Ken Gire*

Believe God has a purpose for you
Understand how He wants to use you
Integrate His plan into your life
Love and live for Him each day
Devote and dedicate your focus to Him

Haggai 1:7-8
"Thus says the Lord of Hosts: 'Consider your ways! Go up to the mountains and bring wood and build the temple, that I may take pleasure in it and be glorified,' says the Lord." (NKJV)

The people had started building the temple in Jerusalem and lost interest after only 1 month. People around them had made fun of their efforts. It didn't compare to the beauty and quality of Solomon's temple, so the people became discouraged. Instead, they began working on their own paneled houses. For 16 years they ignored the task they had been assigned to do from God, and put all their energies in their own accomplishments. Even though their houses were beautiful and they were doing well in life, they weren't satisfied...something was missing in their lives.

Haggai, the prophet, was sent as a messenger to encourage the people to come back and finish what had been started. This would be the fulfillment they were desiring.

He had 3 messages from the Lord.
1) **Consider your ways**
2) **Be strong and work**
3) **I will bless you**

What is your assignment from God? Do you know?
Have you allowed someone to discourage you?
Have you started the assignment God has given you?
Have you completed it?
What is the next assignment?
Do you know?

Finish what God has assigned to you.
Finish what has been started.

Your thoughts...

FOCUS

Find
Outcomes
Centered
Upon the
Spirit

"Nothing can add more power to your life than concentrating all your energies on a limited set of targets."

Niido Quebien

Isaiah 61:1
"The Spirit of the Lord God is upon me, because the Lord has anointed me to preach good tidings to the poor; He has sent me to heal the brokenhearted, to proclaim liberty to the captives, and the opening of the prison to those who are bound." (NKJV)

You are a child of the living God!

You can do anything through the power of His Holy Spirit. All you have to do is believe this truth and focus on what your purpose and passion is. Determine to stay focused and take steps in that direction.

With the help of the Holy Spirit, you will see the gifts He has created in you.

You will see His touch and His passion unfold in the journey He purposed.

You will see how divine it is in you.

Keep your focus on Him.

Your thoughts…

FOLLOW

Find
Out the
Lord's mission–
Live
Out His
Word

*"The immature mind hops from one thing to another;
the mature mind seeks to follow through."*

Harry A. Overstreet

Ezekiel 20:19-20
"I am the Lord your God; follow my decrees and be careful to keep my laws. Keep my Sabbaths holy, that they may be a sign between us. Then you will know that I am the Lord your God." (NIV)

When you know what you want in life, it's just a matter of going after it. If it is money, we invest in activities and employment that will produce it. If it is recognition and status, our choices will always have ourselves in the limelight. If it is a life of serving ourselves, our life will be focused on activities that bring only us pleasure. On the other hand, if our life is dedicated to our Creator, we strive to know Him more, to understand His mission and purpose.

As we follow Him, our lives reflect His purpose, not ours.

As we follow Him, we think more like Him.

As we follow Him, our actions and reactions mirror Him.

Your thoughts...

SERVE

Study and know God's Word
Exercise His ways
Reach out to others
Vitalize the purpose
Extend the love of God

"The best servant does his work unseen."

Oliver Wendell Holmes, Sr. (1809-1894)

Deuteronomy 10:12-13
"And now, Oh Israel, what does the Lord your God ask of you but to fear the Lord your God, to walk in all His ways, to love Him, to serve the Lord your God with all your heart and all your soul, and to observe the Lord's commands and decrees that I am giving you today for your own good?"(NIV)

Serving requires a willingness to do so. So many times we don't think there is anything worthwhile **we** can do. What if the prophets of time felt this way? Recently, I received this anonymous writing reflecting the writer's opinion of their credentials:

Noah was a drunk… Abraham was too old… Isaac was a daydreamer… Jacob was a liar… Joseph was abused… Moses had a stuttering problem… Gideon was afraid… Samson had long hair and was a womanizer… Rahab was a prostitute… Jeremiah and Timothy were too young… David had an affair and was a murderer… Elijah was suicidal… Isaiah preached naked… Jonah ran from God… Naomi was a widow… Job went bankrupt… Peter denied Christ… the Disciples fell asleep while praying… Martha worried about everything… The Samaritan woman was divorced, more than once… Zaccheus was too small… Paul was too religious… Timothy had an ulcer… AND Lazarus was dead!

No more excuses now. God can use YOU! Besides, you aren't the message, you are just the messenger.

Remember, serving is our Mission.

Three Important Points in Serving:

1) God has uniquely created you.
2) God gives us special abilities when we follow Him.
3) Put your spiritual gifts into action. Whatever God has given you– do it well! Very well!

Your thoughts...

SOW

Shelter
Of your
Wings

"Be it ours, when we cannot see the face of God, to trust under the shadow of His wings."

Charles H. Spurgeon

Psalm 61:4
"I long to dwell in your tent forever and take refuge in the shelter of your wings." (NIV)

Picture yourself under the shelter of God's wings. Curled up in His presence, you rest. You are in His care now.

All that you have carried on your shoulders has been lifted. His strong wings have brushed all aside. You are to let Him handle those worries and burdens… You feel safe and cared for. You are not alone. You are in His shelter.

There are times in our life when God knows we need His shelter– complete safety and shelter.

As we take refuge, we rest and heal in our souls. We gain strength to get back on our knees to finally stand again. It is there where God spreads His wings and we walk forward, but never leave His shadow. He is over us at all times. We know He covers us in all we are handling.

Shadow
Of your
Wings

Psalm 36:7
"How priceless is your unfailing love! Both high and low among men finds refuge in the shadow of your wings." (NKJV)

Psalm 57:1
"Be merciful to me, O God, be merciful to me! For my soul trusts in You; And in the shadow of Your wings I will make my refuge, until these calamities have passed by." (NIV)

Whether His shelter or shadow, God is always there.

Your thoughts...

KNOW

> *"Real knowledge, like everything else of value, is not to be obtained easily. It must be worked for, studied for, thought for, and, more than all, must be prayed for."*
>
> *Thomas Arnold*
> *(1795-1842)*

Keep your appointment with the Father
New mercies are fresh every morning
Open your heart to hear
Walk in His presence each day

John 8:31-32
"If you abide in my Word you are my disciples indeed. And you shall know the truth and the truth shall make You free". (NKJV)

How powerful it is to know. To know who you are in Christ makes an incredible difference in a person's life. To know what you are here for. To know that your life is meant to be fulfilling and purposeful. That is the truth.

Do you know?

As the saying goes, "When you know, that you know, that you know... you really know." Do you sway back and forth on what you know? Or does your life, who you are, what you do...stand on what you know and is it firm?

When an observer remarked about the sculpture of a magnificent lion that Michelangelo was sculpting, she asked him how he could carve a lion with such detail and perfection out of stone? The response from Michelangelo indicated that it was not that difficult. He just had to carve away everything that wasn't a lion.

He knew what he was to do. He had a vision and he knew it in detail. God wants us to have a knowing about who we are in Him and what He wants us to do in this lifetime for Him.

Do you know?

Your thoughts…

REAP

Realizing
Everything
Abides in God's
Presence

"No joy on earth is equal to the bliss of being all taken up with love to Christ. If I had my choice of all the lives that I could live, I certainly would not choose to be an emperor, nor to be a millionaire, nor to be a philosopher, for the power and wealth and knowledge bring with them sorrow. But, I would choose to have nothing to do but to love my Lord Jesus–nothing, I mean, but to do all things for his sake, and out of love to him."

Unknown

Galatians 6:9
"And let us not grow weary while doing good, for in due season we shall reap if we do not lose heart." (NKJV)

Charles Stanley states the 1st Life Principle in our lives as; "Our intimacy with God–His highest priority for our lives–Determines the impact of our lives."

Three reasons God seeks our surrender to Him;

1) God loves each of us and desires a relationship with us.
    Isn't this a great privilege?
2) He wants our service for Him to be effective and fruitful.
    What great fulfillment this will bring!
3) He waits for the freedom to bless us.
    Wow! How can we turn this down?

Is God your priority? Is what you are reaping focused on your relationship with Him?

When you are aligned and centered in God's will; all your work, all your efforts, all of your time will reap incredible rewards. As we strive to live in God's spirit, we will reap the fruit of the Spirit in our lives. The nine virtues are: love, joy, peace, patience, kindness, goodness, faithfulness, gentleness, and self-control. Yes, it involves commitment, patience and perseverance, but the fruit of your labor will be sweet—like nothing else.

Your thoughts…

VALUE

Visualize the
Almighty's
Love
Unconditionally
Everyday

"What matters is not the fact that I know God, but the larger fact which underlies it–the fact that He knows me. I am never out of His mind. All my knowledge of Him depends on His sustained initiative in knowing me. I know Him because He first knew me, and continues to know me."

J. I. Packer

Psalm 139:13
"For you formed my inward parts; You covered me in my mother's womb. I will praise You, for I am fearfully and wonderfully made; Marvelous are Your works, and that my soul knows very well." (NKJV)

Do you realize that God values you? He formed you. Think of the love that He has for you. Knowing and understanding that value gives confidence in living our lives to the fullest.

A person who is centered, focused, peaceful and content in their relationship with Christ has a confidence in who they are. As I started looking at this more, I learned it stems from the person feeling valued. When we know we are of value–God's creation and made in His image, it makes a difference in our approach of how we do life. It is easier to trust Him with our life.

I hope you feel valued because God made you uniquely special and cares about you dearly.

Your thoughts…

OBEY

Obedience
Becomes the
Expectation of
You

"Prepare thy soul calmly to obey; such offering will be more acceptable to God than every other sacrifice."

*Metastasio
(pseudonym of Antonio Domenico Bonaventura Trapassi Pietro)*

Romans 2:13
"For it is not those who hear the law who are righteous in God's sight, but it is those who obey the law who will be declared righteous." (NIV)

It is important for us to obey.
5 points that will equip us to be obedient to His commands:

1. Be Submissive—*answer to His authority*
2. Be Obedient—*follow His commands*
3. Be Available—*His call becomes your need*
4. Be Clean and Holy—*consider all your ways*
5. Be Prepared—*have His plan in hand*

I have often found myself confused as I try to do these things, yet I can't figure out why things are not going in a better direction in my life. In the Life Principle Bible by Charles Stanley, he explains that sometimes we may have ignored God or only completed part of what He has asked us to do.

"God does not require us to understand His will, just obey it even if it seems unreasonable." Joshua 3:8 (NKJV)

This makes a lot of sense to me. I have not truly obeyed when I delay His plans or just work them in when it seems convenient to me. I have experienced that through the completion of this book. I have known for a long time that I was to write this book with the "Nuggets" that God had given me. But life kept getting in the way and I put all the reasons of delay around it. My full time job, my grandbabies coming into the world, my financial responsibilities…then it came down to me looking truly at what God wants. I got down on my knees and cried out, "What do you want me to do? I am doing all I can." The message I received back was, "Finish The Book."

As I am doing this, I shake my head not knowing how it is all going to come together, but I know as I do this that I am being obedient. I am doing what I know I am to do and God takes care of the rest.

Obedience always brings blessings.

Your thoughts…

TRACE

Tremendous
Results
Account for
Christ's
Excellence

"God guides us, despite our uncertainties and vagueness, even through our failings and mistakes...He leads us step by step, from event to event.

Only afterwards, as we look back over the way we have come... do we experience the feeling of having been led without knowing it, the feeling that God has mysteriously guided us."

Paul Tournier

Isaiah 42:6
"I the Lord have called you in righteousness, and will hold your hand; I will keep you and give you as a covenant to the people, as a light to the Gentiles." (NKJV)

In the incredible book, "The Power of Jabez," Bruce Wilkerson writes, "Recognize His divine answer. See His path. You will have a front row seat in a life of miracles."

It is important on our journey to see how God has been involved. Sometimes it is difficult to see that when we are told our job is ending in 2 weeks or someone dear to us has been diagnosed with a terminal illness.

But as we trust, we will be able to TRACE–maybe not right at that very moment. Definitely in time, you will be able to trace an evident path and purpose of God's works and intentions.

TRACE His Hand.

Your thoughts…

IMAGINE

In this
Moment
Accept
God's
Intimate
Nature
Everyday

"A man is but the product of his thoughts, what he thinks, he becomes."

Mohandas K. Gandhi
(1869-1948)

Just Imagine
Imagine in your quietness
    that God is sitting right with you

He slowly lifts His arms up toward you

Without saying a word–you lean forward
    and lay your head on His shoulder

You feel His arms wrap around you

His gentle strength is soothing to your soul
    all of a sudden your worries, hurts and fears are released
The calmness from your Savior dissolved the hold on you
    that divided you from receiving complete peace and joy

Now you are set free from all that has held you
He holds you now in the shelter of His wings
You melt in His arms, receiving all you need

He whispers in your ear–
    stay near my child

Just Imagine

Your thoughts…

TRUST

To
Rely
Upon the
Savior
Today

*"Sure it takes a lot of courage,
To put things in God's hands,
To give ourselves completely,
Our lives, our hopes, our plans;
To follow where He leads us,
And make His will our own,
But all it takes is foolishness,
To go the way alone."*

Betsey Kline

2 Samuel 22:2-3
"The Lord is my rock and my fortress and my deliverer; The God of my strength, in whom I will trust; My shield and the horn of my salvation. My stronghold and my refuge; My Savior…"(NKJV)

Trust derives from the Greek word, **chasah** *(chah-sah)*; Strong #2620. It is defined as; to trust, to hope, to make someone a refuge. This verb occurs 36 times in the Old Testament. Psalm 57:1 beautifully illustrates the verb where it pictures David nestling under God's wings for refuge, in the same manner that a defenseless but trusting baby bird hides itself under its parent's feathers. Psalm 118:8 states, "It is better to trust ***(chasah)*** in the Lord than to put confidence in man," a fitting centerpiece of the Bible.

It is so hard to trust, especially when it hits close to us. When things are completely out of our control, it seems like there is nothing we can do but worry. It is at this time when God is teaching us to rely on Him, not ourselves or someone else. It is a time to "Let Go, Let God."

Do you have a situation in your life right now where God may be saying, "My daughter/son, nestle under my wings and let me handle this for you? Just trust me."

Reflect on the quote of Meister Eckhart (AD 1260-1328) stating: "God expects but one thing of you, and that is that you…Let God be God in you."

What if you do that right now? Close your eyes and tell Him that you know He is your Rock, your Savior. Let Him be God in you.

Your thoughts…

PART III

THESE REQUIRE YOUR IMMEDIATE ATTENTION

Nuggets to be aware of

"As long as you keep a person down, some part of you has to be down, so it means you cannot soar as you otherwise might."

Marian Anderson
(1902-1993)

DOUBT

Delayed results
Obstacles remain
Unlimited Limits
Belief is not there
Trust is not evident

"If the Sun and Moon should doubt, they'd immediately go out."

William Blake (1757-1827)

James 1:5
"But let him ask in faith, with no doubting, for he who doubts is like a wave of the sea driven and tossed by the wind." (NKJV)

I remember my mentor telling me that "Doubt causes delay." It is so true.

If we doubt ourselves, we are causing limitations to occur. On the other hand, if we believe with confidence–we can accomplish anything we put our mind to. Doubt slows you down and can be an obstacle in accomplishing what could be an incredible opportunity for you.

I have a friend I've known for over 10 years and the thing that surprised me the most was that doubt ruled over her like a cloud. She had a lot of things going okay in her life, but it was only a fraction of what she could be experiencing. After spending time really getting to know her, I learned a lot of her doubt stemmed from her relationship with her mother. Her mother always had a negative attitude toward her causing her to feel that she never measured up.

It took awhile to figure it out because I would ask her what her goals were, and they were never much more than where she was. She really didn't believe that she could own a house at that stage in her life because she really couldn't see making enough money in her position to do so. I remember asking her what she wanted to make in salary and she had a hard time stating a number. I remember throwing out a number about $6,000 higher than she was thinking. She responded with, "There is no way that would work at our place of employment." Do you know after a few months she changed her way of thinking and less than 2 years later she was making that number?

She believed.

Your thoughts...

FEAR

False
Evidence that
Appears
Real

*"Whenever I feel afraid
 I hold my head erect
And whistle a happy tune
So no one will suspect
I'm afraid...*

*The result of this deception
Is very strange to tell,
For when I fool the people I fear
I fool myself as well!"*

Oscar Hammerstein II

Haggia 2:5
"According to the Word that I coveted with you when you came out of Egypt, so My Spirit remains among you, do not fear." (NKJV)

The Hebrew word for fear is ***phobeo***; Strong #5399. The definition is to be frightened, dismayed, and described as panic that causes one to run away. God does not want us to have a phobia of men or things, as this can be debilitating or even destructive.

What are your fears? Fear of rejection or failure? Fear of what you know are your weaknesses? Fear of past hurts? Fear of death?

Are you living in fear? Or, are you living in faith?

Begin today by starting to identify your fears. Once you do that, you can pray diligently about them with your heavenly Father. He will dissolve your fears as you follow Him in faith.

Take an extra dose of God's Word to guard you against fear:

1 John 4:18
"There is no fear in love; but perfect love casts out fear, because fear involves torment. But he who fears has not been made perfect in love." (NKJV)

Reflect on the knowing that perfect love casts out fear.

2 Timothy 1:7
"For God has not given us a spirit of fear, but of power and of love and of a sound mind." (NKJV)

Reflect on the knowing that being filled with God's Spirit will cause you to become fearless.

Your thoughts…

ANGER

Admit your anger
No action to follow
Get away–Go to God
Examine the cause
Redirect your anger

"I always throw my golf clubs in the direction I'm going."

Ronald Reagan (1911-2005)

Ephesians 4:26
"Be angry and do not sin. Let not the sun go down on your wrath."
(NKJV)

In the concordance of my Bible regarding this verse, it is stated that being angry may win a moment, but anger is not to be allowed to win a day.

I was very surprised when I learned that anger is a God-given emotion, right along with love and compassion. I always thought of it as a bad thing. I prided myself that it wasn't something I struggled with. But, as I have gone through tough experiences and as I get older, I am seeing more of this emotion in me.

I am learning through God's Word that anger is not necessarily sinful. Anger must have safe grounds. We are instructed not to let the sun go down and still be angry. Find resolution. Secondly, don't allow Satan to take over in the moment of anger. Phyllis Diller had her own rendition of this verse. She said that we should never let the sun go down angry… instead stay up and fight!

Remember, anger is only one letter away from Danger.

Dr. David Jeremiah speaks an incredible message on anger, "Slaying the Giant of Anger." He reminds us that Jesus' anger was never about something that was done to him. His anger was righteous anger on the right grounds for the right reasons. He reminds us that we should learn to deal with our anger. In doing this, we should not rehearse our anger. He feels that no one can make you angry–they just bring it out in you. Don't let your mouth be your source of promoting anger. Proverbs 22:24-25 says not to be around an angry man or person. It will affect you.

As you go forward, have a forgiving spirit, as God teaches us to do and not a spirit of anger. God could have easily poured out his anger upon all of us but instead His Son carried it all. May you have release of any anger that is within you today.

Your thoughts...

FOG

Forgetting to
Obey
God

"The remarkable truth is that our choices matter, not just to us and our own destiny but, amazingly, to God Himself and the universe He rules."

Philip Yancey

Proverbs 28:26
"He who trusts in his own heart is a fool, but whoever walks wisely will be delivered." (NKJV)

I remember one day driving through incredible fog on my way to work. I couldn't see the car in front or behind me. I felt as if I was blinded. All I had to go on was the path that I knew was right. It would have been easy to veer to the right or left exit without knowing if I was on the right road. It would have been easy to end up in the ditch. I prayed that the fog would lift, so there would not be anything that would block my vision.

Disobedience, like heavy fog, can lead us astray, off course–right into a ditch. Often, right before the Lord delivers a breakthrough, Satan makes it the most difficult. The fog becomes heavy and if we do not stay on track and ask for His guidance, the breakthrough we were about to receive does not come or is delayed.

As we obey God, things become clearer. Confusion and doubt lift like a fog that diminishes right before our eyes. We keep our focus, see clearly before us and know God's direction.

Where are you right now? Can you see clearly or have you allowed the fog to creep in?

Your thoughts…

SECRETS

Satan abides
Exceptions allowed
Closet of poison
Regrets continue
Excuses given
Truth is hidden
Strive to cover

"There must be some narrowness in the soul that compels one to have secrets."

Henry David Thoreau
(1817-1862)

Luke 8:17
"For nothing is secret that will not be revealed, nor anything hidden that will not be known and come to light." (NKJV)

Pray for truth in every situation that you are dealing with. Pray that everything that is hidden be revealed. Are you concerned that deception is in the midst of someone's life that is intertwined with you? Do you have concerns that someone's secrets are going to affect someone you hold dear to your heart?

What are the secrets you are holding on to? Could they hurt someone or those dear to you? Are they blocking you from receiving what God has for you? Make sure you don't deceive yourself with your own secrets.

Call it what it truly is–not covering any part of it.

Your thoughts…

ALONE

Agonizing
Lonely
Oppressive
Negative
Empty

Avenue to
Learn more about
Ourselves–
Need to
Experience who we are in God

"We need others. We need others to love and we need to be loved by them. There is no doubt that without it, we too, like the infant left alone, would cease to grow, cease to develop, choose madness and even death."

Leo F. Buscaglia
(1924-1998)

"All of our unhappiness comes from our inability to be alone."

Jean de la Bruyere

John 16:32c
"Yet I am not alone, for my Father is with me." (NKJV)

Loneliness can be painful. It is important to know that in those experiences, God is with you always. Loneliness is felt by many in our world. It can be felt through the loss of a spouse, partner, parent or child in your life. Maybe a devastating tragedy has affected you or your family, and changed everything for you. All of a sudden you feel alone. Results and emotions of a broken relationship, living in an area now with no family or friends in sight or faced with insurmountable issues that you feel are on you alone, can result in loneliness.

Loneliness can also be felt in the midst of many surrounding you, having acquired much and the appearance of everything being perfect. Yet, loneliness tugs at your heart with a heaviness and strong desire to have fulfillment or peace that is not present. Although not appearing lonely, your heart screams out with pains of emptiness.

On the other hand, the ultimate of being alone in any and every situation is understanding and knowing that God is always there and finding comfort in that knowing. God is our refuge and strength andwith us always–no matter what. Being alone no longer means pain and heartache. Instead, it is a time for us to know God and learn about who we are in Him. It is a time to let Him lead us, showing us that He cares about our situation and will see us through.

Your thoughts…

PRIDE

Personal gain
Relevant to "me"
"I" not we
Diminishes love
Ego thrives

"A proud man is always looking down on things and people; and, of course, as long as you're looking down, you can't see something that's above you."

C. S. Lewis
(1898-1963)

Proverbs 29:23
"A man's pride will bring him low, but the humble in spirit will retain honor." (NKJV)

The Hebrew word for pride is ***huperephania***. It means haughtiness, arrogance and a disdainful attitude toward others. In Mark 7:21-22, pride is 12th on the list of 13 inner vices. Being proud holds you back. When you are proud, you can't receive like you could with an open or humble heart. Instead of a heart of pride, we are to have a meek heart as Jesus did.

Creflo Dollar refers to pride as the ultimate blessing blocker. He explains that pride is when you trust in your own words, plan, abilities and will–ignoring God's words, plan, abilities and will. Creflo asks us who drew the blueprint of your life? You or God? He states that where there is pride, there is going to be a fall.

I remember reading about the King of Tyre who was being humbled because he was so full (fool) of himself. Although he was full of wisdom and beauty, yet full of pride–God brought him down.

Self-centeredness is the essence of worldliness. It is not a focus on God.

Your thoughts…

SIN

Satan
Invades
Nearby

"Sin is whatever obscures the soul."

Andre Gide

John 1:29
"The next day John saw Jesus coming toward him, and said, 'Behold! The Lamb of God who takes away the sin of the world!'" (NKJV)

Sin derives from the Greek word, ***havarti***. It means to miss the mark, take the wrong course or wrongdoing. Sin separates us from God. I remember a pastor that explained it this way; "Sin weakens your reason."

The Lord requires commitment from His people. When we commit sin, the Lord in His love, chastises us until we come to full repentance. When we cry out to Him, the Lord faithfully responds to us. He forgives us, brings deliverance to us, and restores fellowship with us. (NKJV)

Think of a target in front of you. The center is all that God stands for. What He calls us to do and be–that's the bull's eye. When we do not do what He commands, we miss the mark. We miss God's best for us when we sin. (NKJV)

Your thoughts…

WAR

We
Are
Regressing

"There was never a good war or a bad peace."

Benjamin Franklin (1706-1790)

1 Samuel 17:45
"Then David said to the Philistine, 'You come to me with a sword, with a spear, and with a javelin. But I come to you in the name of the Lord of hosts, the God of the armies of Israel, whom you have defied.'" (NKJV)

When I first wrote this word, I was only thinking about the wars between God's people. I remember hearing my Dad mention the 3 wars he served in, but never knew much more than that. Later in my life, I got a close look of what war can do to someone as I experienced it firsthand from someone who was a survivor but suffered greatly in their daily life from the traumatic affects of the war. In my experience, this person in my life lost their life in more ways than one to the war. Soon after I included this in the book, we went to war in Iraq. We also have the horrible memories of 9/11 that demonstrate war right among us. What a controversial subject that could lend itself to debate after debate!

Whether it is a major war between countries, states, parties or people– war signifies division and separation. As I look at war around us, I can also see the battles that we deal with daily.

Just recently, I heard Joyce Meyer share her thoughts on those times of battle in our lives. She used the scripture above to demonstrate what we should do. She gave the visual picture of David headed right toward Goliath prophesying his defeat. He was speaking it out before it occurred. It was great picturing David running toward the battle line. Joyce stated that we have to learn how to enjoy life while we have problems. We need to acknowledge that it is okay to trust. As Joyce was speaking, it made me reflect on what issues in my life are at hand right now. How can I get to a place to get my confession in the now?

We are so tempted to believe that if we don't see anything, God is not doing anything. Learn to recognize that God is here now. Right in the middle of the battle.

Don't quit. The middle is the battle and it determines our finish. How we handle our battles shows more about us in life. How we handle our disappointments. How we handle our enemies. Don't speak or act in fear. Instead, go to battle in faith believing that God will prevail.

We need to be very careful when we are in a battle, and try not to win the battle mentally. Instead, worship and praise yourself through it.

Your thoughts…

PAIN

Penetrating
Agony
Increasing
Need

"He who has been delivered from pain must not think he is now free again, and at liberty to take life up just as it was before, entirely forgetful of the past. He is now a 'man whose eyes are open' with regard to pain and anguish, and he must help to overcome those two enemies (so far as human power can overcome them) and to bring the others the deliverance which he has himself enjoyed."

*Albert Schweitzer
(1875-1965)
The Experiences and Observations of a Doctor in Equatorial Africa*

Psalm 139:1-3, 5, 7-10, 13, 15-16
"O Lord, you have searched me and know me. You know when I sit and when I rise; you perceive my thought from afar. You discern my going out and my lying down; you are familiar with all my ways. You hem me in–behind and before; you have laid your hand upon me.
Where can I go from your Spirit?
Where can I flee from your presence?
If I go up to the heavens, you are there; if I make my bed in the depths, you are there. If I rise on the wings of the dawn, if I settle on the far side of the sea, even there your hand will guide me, your right hand will hold me fast. For you created my inmost being; you knit me together in my mother's womb. My frame was not hidden from you when I was made in the secret place. When I was woven together in the depths. Of the earth your eyes saw my unformed body. All the days ordained for me were written in your book before one of them came to be." (NIV)

Pain...deep pain...is penetrating to our being. There is nothing like it. When we are in deep pain, the world changes around us. I remember meeting with a gentleman regarding my book and as he requested examples of the Nuggets, this word, PAIN, came up. He began to share his pain with me. He and his wife had lost 2 of their children. The pain in this man's eyes was gut wrenching. The discovery of cancer or illness with frightening unknowns, physical pain that stops you from enjoying life, pain from the heart of broken dreams—all these situations allow God to swoop down and carry us on His wings.

As we remember that God knows our pain to the detail, we are to rely on Him to carry us, heal us, and teach us through the experience.

Your thoughts...

The Dirty D's

Deception
Distraction
Disinterest
Detours
Dishonesty
Dependency
Discouragement
Dissatisfaction
Depression
Destruction

"Everything that exalts and expands consciousness is good, while that which depresses and diminishes, it is evil."
Miguel de Unamuno (1864-1936)

"Every human being has two inclinations—one prompting him to good... and the other prompting him to evil...; but the Divine assistance is near, and he who asks the help of God in contending with the evil promptings of his own heart obtains it."
Muhammad (A.D 570-632)

"The meaning of good and bad.... is simply helping or hurting."
Ralph Waldo Emerson (1803-1882)

Isaiah 41:10
"So do not fear, for I am with you; do not be dismayed, for I am your God. I will strengthen you and help you; I will uphold you with my righteous right hand." (NIV)

Have any of these ever affected you? How many of them have you had to deal with? They can get in the way of God's plan for us. That's why my mentor calls them the Dirty D's.

God is a God of truth not deception. He will guide us and help us to stay focused. He has so much to offer in our lives. He may allow us to slip, but not fall. He wants us to be encouraged, to see His hope, to see our future in Him. He wants to expand our life in the most fulfilling way.

He is a God that creates, loves, builds, restores.

Watch out for the Dirty D's. Through **prayer and meditation** the Dirty D's will **Disappear!**

Your thoughts…

PART IV

HOLD THESE DEAR TO YOUR HEART

Nuggets to cherish

"*I believe we shall in some manner be cherished by our Maker–that the One who gave us this remarkable earth has the power still farther to surprise that which He has caused beyond that which all is silence.*"

Emily Dickinson (1830-1886)

CORE

Christ is the center
Of my life
Relying on Him for
Everything

*"His center is everywhere,
His circumference is nowhere."*

Henry Law

Philippians 4:13
"I can do all things through Christ who strengthens me." (NKJV)

I remember when I was struggling to get balance in my life. I tried continually to keep some margin in my life. I began evaluating commitments I had made and addressed the priority I was giving them.

What I have come to realize is this; if I stay centered in Christ, the balance comes. I won't be I-centered. How I choose my activities is much more effective. When Jesus is the center of my life, a core of everything He represents is evident. As I live in this core–the essence of Christ radiates out in everything I or you do.

It pleasantly affects your family and home environment.
It gracefully affects your relationships across the board.
It significantly affects your work, finances and interests.
It amazingly becomes your ministry.

Your thoughts…

SHIELD

Savior
Help
Intercessor
Exterminator
Leader
Deliverer

"The will of God will never take you to where the grace of God will not protect you. To gain that which is worth having, it may be necessary to lose everything else."

Charles Stanley

Psalm 5:12
"For you, O Lord, will bless the righteous; with favor You will surround him as with a shield." (NKJV)

God is our shield. He is our Savior and Help in any and every situation. He acts as our personal intercessor. He has the power of an exterminator to eliminate obstacles in our life. As our leader, he protects us and delivers us from trouble, controversy, pain and whatever the world may bring to us.

Daniel is a great example of how God is a shield for us. From Daniel's humble beginning of serving as a trainee in Nebuchadnezzar's court, to later becoming an advisor to foreign kings–he learned to depend on God's guidance, protection and deliverance.

Is God your shield? Do you allow Him to help you? Do you believe in His power to intercede, deliver and lead you in the walk ahead? He is a mighty steadfast shield–He wants to be first and foremost in our lives.

Your thoughts…

REAL

Relationship Not Religion
Equality Not Discrimination
Acceptance Not Division
Love Not Judgment

"O God help us not to despise what we do not understand."

William Penn

Isaiah 66:18
"For I know their works and their thoughts. It shall be that I will gather all nations and tongues and they shall come and see my glory." (NKJV)

I love to think of how real God is.

It helps me realize He is there for me to depend on. Sometimes we make God to be complex. I think He loves simplicity and truth. In Isaiah 1:18 it is written, "Come now and let us reason together," says the Lord. (NIV) He is a real God based on principles of love, truth and salvation for ALL people.

How different would our world be if we strived to be REAL?

I recently viewed an incredible photo of Earth from space that was taken Christmas Eve, 1968 during Apollo 8. The photograph was taken by rookie, Bill Anders. Upon studying this photo closely, Archibald MacLeish wrote:

"To see the earth as it truly is, small and blue and beautiful in that eternal silence where it floats, is to see ourselves as riders on the earth together, brothers on that bright loveliness in the eternal cold–brothers that know they are truly brothers."

Your thoughts…

PRESENCE

Personal
Relationship
Experiencing God's
Spirit–the
Essence of His
Nearness &
Closeness is
Exhilarating

"When we stray from His presence, He longs for you to come back. He weeps that you are missing out on His love, protection and provision. He throws His arms open, runs toward you, gathers you up, and welcomes you home."

Unknown

Exodus 33:14
"And He said, 'My Presence will go with you, and I will give you rest.'" (NKJV)

What does it mean to have God's presence with you? How do we become in His presence? In Exodus 33, Moses pitched his tent far from the camp, called it the tabernacle of meeting and went there alone to meet with God. When he entered the tabernacle, the pillar of cloud descended and stood at the door. There the Lord spoke to Moses.

When we enter God's presence, it is peaceful and restful. It is exhilarating and powerful. It is a personal, intimate experience with our God. Surrounded by truth and filled with love, we experience His closeness as we draw close to Him.

Just as Moses did, we can speak face to face with God. Moses even replied questioning God further. I like that part. I always want to know more, and that's exactly what Moses did. He prayed, "If I have found grace in Your sight, show me now Your way, that I may know You and that I may find grace in Your sight." (vs. 13)

Entering in God's presence allows us to have direction from Him personally. His favor is extended to us. Pray Moses' prayer, asking God to show you His way so that you may know Him and have His grace.

Your thoughts…

PROMISE

Provides His **P**resence
Reveals **R**estoration
Opens **O**pportunities
Moves **M**ountains
Inspires and **I**nstructs
Sends the **S**pirit
Extends **E**ncouragement

"Life Is A Promise–Fulfill It."

Mother Teresa

2 Peter 3:13
"Nevertheless, we according to His promise, look for new heavens and a new earth in which righteousness dwells." (NKJV)

God's promise to us is so precious. It is a privilege to know that His promises are true and forever reliable. It is important that each one of us understands what God's promise means in our life.

The word promise derives from the word ***epangelia*** *(ep-ang-el-ee-ah)*; Strong #1860. It describes the meaning as both a promise and the thing promised, an announcement with the special sense of promise, pledge, and offer. ***Epangelia*** tells what the promise from God is, and also gives the assurance that the thing promised will be done. In 2 Corinthians 1:20 it states, "For all the promises, ***espangelia***, of God in Him are Yes, and in Him Amen, to the glory of God through us."

God's promises are true.
God's promises are reliable.
God's promises are for you.

As we go through this walk, disappointments and heartbreaks occur. Situations arise that you never, never thought you would have to go through or deal with. It is then, that we understand what God's promises mean, how they affect the circumstance that we are dealing with, and give us the confidence to walk through it.

His promise means he is ever present for us at this time.
He will show you how to get through it and not crumble.
He will bring signs of hope right before your very eyes.
He will help move the mountain or help you climb over it.
He will inspire, encourage and instruct you all the way.
He will send his sweet holy spirit to see you through.

I dedicate this page to my daughter, Morgan, as she faces a life challenge ahead of her.

Your thoughts...

WORD

Work
Of the Holy Spirit
Righteously
Directed

"Thy Word is a lamp unto my feet and a light unto my path."

Psalms 19:105

Matthew 4:3-4
"Now when the tempter came to him He said, 'If you are the Son of God, command that these stones become bread.' But He answered and said, 'It is written. Man shall not live by bread alone but by every Word that proceeds from the mouth of God.'" (NKJV)

Word derives from the Greek word, ***Theopneustos,*** which literally means; God breathed or the inspiration of God. God's Word is given to us as a tool. It is complete and was planned by the Holy Spirit. In II Timothy 3:16-17, when Paul is defining the scriptures, he states that the Word is our instruction for righteousness so that we may be complete, thoroughly equipped for every good work.

What a beautiful, incredible gift God gives us right at our fingertips.

Your thoughts…

SOAR

Shadow
Of the
Almighty
Reigns

"Refuse to be average. Let your heart soar as high as it will."

Unknown

Isaiah 40:31
"But those who wait upon the Lord shall renew their strength. They shall mount up with wings like eagles, they shall run and not be weary. They shall walk and not faint." (NKJV)

Don't go out of His shadow. The Almighty will come through for you. He will give you everything you need.

His Power.
His Strength.
His Grace.
His Joy.
His Peace.
His Love.

The Almighty reigns above all.

Your thoughts…

LET

Live
Embracing
Trust in God

"When you cannot trust God you cannot trust anything, and when you cannot trust anything, you get the condition of the world as it is today."

Basil King

Matthew 6:26
"Look at the birds of the air, for they neither sow nor reap nor gather into barns; yet your heavenly father feeds them. Are you not of more value than they?" (NKJV)

After a long awaited move, I was excited to know that our new residence was next to a bird sanctuary. What may have bothered others–all the bird talk, constant motion and even odors that come with it–didn't concern us at all. In fact we enjoyed their chatter and loved watching the activity of the "birds of the air." And, we learned to live with the aroma that seemed to come by from time to time.

We learned the Seabird Sanctuary is the largest bird hospital in the world. These 600 birds are cared for according to the degree of their need. The area closest to our home was for the birds that are free to fly in and out as they want. I could count 50 pelicans in a couple of seconds. As I worked in my office, I often found myself watching them.

One day I received a call from a customer who had decided she was satisfied with the older product she purchased from us, and did not want to purchase the new system. I was glad to know our product was successful, but I was looking forward to my first sell. All of a sudden–I looked up and asked God, "You are going to help me make this business work aren't you Lord? You know, I'm taking a big step in faith."

About the time I finished my question, the birds in view started stirring up activity and flying around within their space.

I stared at them and felt God's comforting voice say, "Deb, look at the birds of the air everyday and know I take care of them regardless of the degree of need. I will take care of you far more."

"Just Let Me."

Your thoughts…

PASSION

Purposeful
Affirmation
Signifying the work of the
Spirit–
Increasing
One's
Need and direction

"Passion, it lies in all of us, sleeping... waiting... and though unwanted... unbidden... it will stir... open its jaws and howl. It speaks to us... guides us... passion rules us all, and we obey. What other choice do we have? Passion is the source of our finest moments. The joy of love... the clarity of hatred... and the ecstasy of grief. It hurts more sometimes than we can bear. If we could live without passion maybe we would know some kind of peace... but we would be... empty rooms shuttered and dank. Without passion we'd be truly dead."

Joss Whedon

Colossians 1:9-13
"For this reason we also, since the day we heard it, do not cease to pray for you, and to ask that you may be filled with the knowledge of His will in all wisdom and spiritual understanding; that you may walk worthy of the Lord, fully pleasing Him, being fruitful in every good work and increasing in the knowledge of God; strengthened with all might, according to his glorious power for all patience and longsuffering with joy; giving thanks to the Father who has qualified us to be partakers of the inheritance of the saints in the light. He has delivered us from the power of darkness and conveyed us into the kingdom of the Son of His love." (NKJV)

What are your passions in your life?
For Paul, Christ was the sum and substance of life.

To preach Christ was his consuming passion. To know Him was his highest aspiration and to suffer for Him was a privilege. His chief desire for readers was that they might have the mind of Christ. This was Paul's passion.

What is your passion? How can God be glorified in the passions that you have?

Your thoughts...

ARM

Almighty
Reigns
Mightily

"Walk boldly and wisely...there is a hand above that will help you on."

Philip James Bailey

Psalm 89:13
"You have a mighty arm,
Strong is your hand and high is your right hand,
Righteousness and justice are the foundation of your throne,
Mercy and truth go before your face." (NKJV)

Isaiah 52:10
"The Lord has made bare His holy arm in the eyes of all the nations; and all the ends of the earth shall see the salvation of our God." (NKJV)

Find comfort in God's Word as you picture God's hand and arm. Picture Him rolling up His sleeves. Strong and mighty overseeing us. Yet, gentle and caring, providing for us. Think of God's hand and arm signifying work accomplished.

Isaiah 40:10-11a
"Behold the Lord God shall come with a strong hand, and His arm shall rule for Him. Behold His reward is with Him, and His work before Him. He shall feed His flock like a shepherd. He will gather the lambs with His arm." (NKJV)

Let God work with His hand and arm in your life providing all that you need. Trust Him. Let Him have authority over you.

Psalm 44:3
"For they did not gain possession of the land by their own sword. Nor did their own arm save them. But it was your right arm. Your arm, and the light of your countenance, because you favored them." (NKJV)

Reach up for His arm. It is mighty.

Your thoughts…

SPIRIT

Savior's
Presence
Intervenes
Revealing & Restoring–
Instilling
Truths of God

"You can't win over the devil with physical force, with human influence, with scientific skill, with money, with arguments, or threats or promises. It takes spiritual armor and weapons provided by God and Him alone."

Unknown

Zechariah 4:6
"So he answered and said to me: 'This is the word of the Lord to Zerubbabel; Not by might, nor by power but by My Spirit.'" (NIV)

The word Spirit, derives from two Greek words, ***pneuma*** and ***ruach.***

The definition of ***pneuma*** is explained as a breath, breeze, a current of air, or wind. It is also described as a part of a person capable of responding to God.

Rauch, is described as "The breath of life." It can be a human spirit, a distressing spirit or the Spirit of God.

As it is written in Zechariah, the essence is that Zerubbabel will complete the temple project "by my Spirit." God's Spirit.

What projects do you have before you that are God's plan for you to complete? You may not know how in the world you are going to accomplish the task at hand but know if you are obedient and apply yourself, God's Spirit will do the rest.

Your thoughts…

ANGELS

*"Around our pillows
golden ladders rise,
And up and down the skies,
With winged sandals shod,
The angels come, and go,
 the Messengers of God."*

*Richard Henry Stoddard
(1825-1903)*

Always bless the Lord in worship & service-1
Never cease to do His work here on earth-2
Get the true message from God first-3
Excel in strength (bonus)
Listen and heed the word of God-4
Stand all around us to do God's pleasure-5

Psalm 91:11
"For He shall give his angels charge over you.
 To keep you in all your ways." (NKJV)

There has been so much written and illustrated regarding angels over the last several years. I decided my source to understand God's angels must be His Word. As I sought to know what God's purpose for his angels were, I learned about his five-fold ministry for angels. The Nugget above describes what God's Word shows us. It put it all in perspective for me.

A friend of mine also shared a nugget about angels that is truly a summary of my study. This nugget is wonderful for children or for those that need a quick reminder of God's chosen ones to guide and protect us.

Always
Near
Guiding
Each
Life
Silently

Psalm 34:7 comes to mind.
"The angel of the world encamps all around those who fear Him and delivers them." (NKJV)

Your thoughts…

PART V

PLAN YOUR WORK, WORK YOUR PLAN

Nuggets to deliver

"God is in me. I am in God. I want Him. I seek Him… I hope to improve myself. I do not know how to, but I feel that God will help all those who seek Him. I am a seeker, for I can feel God. God seeks me and therefore we will find each other."

Vaslav Nijinsky

WILL

Whatever
Is the
Lord's
Love

"We are responsible human beings, not blind automatons, persons not puppets. By endowing us with freedom, God relinquished a measure of His own sovereignty and imposed certain limitations upon Himself. If His children are free, they must do His will by a voluntary choice."

Martin Luther King, Jr.
(1929-1968)

Psalm 143:10
"Teach me to do Your will, for You are my God; Your Spirit is good. Lead me into the land of uprightness." (NKJV)

This is a tough one for me at times. It means that I have to let go completely and let God show me His will in the situation. In doing this, I think of it as an opportunity to trust His love for me.

Just like the times as parents, we tell our children that we are making this decision for their good. That in time…they will see…

God wants more for us than we can imagine for ourselves. That is because His love for us is great! He sees the big picture.

Whatever you are hoping or waiting for–trust God to bring about the outcome He wills. God's will is good, pleasing and perfect.

Your thoughts…

HIS

Hear His Voice
Instill His Words
See His Plan

"When I look at the galaxies on a clear night—when I look at the incredible brilliance of creation, and think that this is what God is like, then instead of feeling intimidated and diminished by it, I am enlarged—I rejoice that I am part of it."

Madeline L. Engle

Psalm 73:23
"Yet I am always with you; you hold me by my right hand. You guide me with your counsel, and afterward you take me into glory." (NIV)

When you are His....you can hear Him. As you listen and seek Him, you will begin to see His plan.

It all begins when we realize that God is always with us and will never leave us. That's the secret. When we truly believe that God is who He says He is; we will see His touch, feel His grace, and experience His love. Are you His? Do you believe that God is with you? Do you want to be His completely? Stop right now and tell Him you want to belong to Him—not this world.

Tell God that you want to hear His voice today. Read Psalms 73:23 out loud and claim His words. As you let go, God will draw you near. He will show you His plan.

Your thoughts…

WAIT

Willingly
Acknowledge the Lord is faithful,
In His
Timing–not ours

"A man watches his pear tree day after day, impatient for the ripening of the fruit. Let him attempt to force the ripening of the fruit, and he may spoil both fruit and tree. But let him patiently wait, and the ripe pear at length falls into his lap!"

Abraham Lincoln (1809-1865)

Lamentations 3:25
"The Lord is good to those who wait for Him, to the soul who seeks Him." (NKJV)

Wait on God. Wait silent and still.
Wait, attentive and responsive. Learn that trust precedes faith.
Exercising your faith in God will help you wait.

I know I am impatient, Lord,
I want to run ahead;
Speak to my heart and make me
Willing to be led.
Your clock is always right Lord.
It never does run late,
Your schedule can't be hurried
So teach me, Lord, to wait.

Your time is never my time–
Oh, make this plain to me
And give me patience so to wait
And Thy fulfillment see.
I see through a glass darkly
And in this earthly state
I only know impatience,
So teach me Lord to wait.

Unknown

Your thoughts…

FEAR

Fear of
Evolving
Awe and
Respect

"I fear God, yet am not afraid of Him."

Sir Thomas Browne

Proverbs 14:26
"In the fear of the Lord there is strong confidence, and His children will have a place of refuge."(NKJV)

We are to have the type of fear that is of reverence and of respect to our mighty God. Not fear that taps into doubt and lack of confidence, but fear that is of the utmost awe and submissive service. A healthy fear.

God's Word tells us that "the fear of the Lord is the beginning of knowledge" (Prov.1:7) and the "beginning of wisdom." (Prov. 9:10)

Our God is a mighty God! May we stand in awe of Him.

Your thoughts...

DEPTH

Discipline to
Engage and
Passion
To know
Him more

"For God Himself works in our souls, in their deepest depths, taking increasing control as we are progressively willing to be prepared for His wonder."

Thomas R. Kelly

James 4:9
"Draw near to God and He will draw near to you." (NKJV)

People are sharp and intuitive. They can read us quickly. It is our depth that will be a great witness to others. If we are shallow, it shows quickly. If we have depth to our spirituality–it becomes intriguing and somewhat mysterious. People are drawn to us and want to know more.

Depth in our personal relationship with Christ can be achieved by studying His Word while reflecting and applying His principles. We become less about "us" and more about "Him."

As we seek the depth in our relationship with God–we know Him intimately.

Your thoughts…

TAG

Truth
And
Grace

"It is the grace of God that helps those do everything that lies within their power to achieve that which is beyond their power."

Abraham Joshua Herschel (1907-1972)

John 1:14
"The word became flesh and made His dwelling among us! We have seen His glory, the glory of the one and only, who came from the Father, full of Grace and Truth." (NIV)

TAG IT! Find the truth in the situation and God's grace will cover it. Truth and grace. They stand together.

In any and every situation, identify what you know to be the truth. Whether it be small or quite evident to see–TAG IT! Respond to what you know to be the truth. God's grace will begin to flow and more truth will be revealed. Maybe you don't know exactly what to do or how to respond. Think about how God would respond.

That is the truth. Grace will follow.

And when truth and grace are woven together–amazing things will happen.

POP

Power
Of
Prayer

"Prayer is an invitation to God to intervene in our lives."

Abraham Joshua Herschel
(1907-1972)

Philippians 4:6
"Be anxious for nothing, but in everything by prayer and supplication, with Thanksgiving, let your requests be known to God; and the peace of God, which surpasses all understanding, will guard your hearts and minds through Christ Jesus." (NKJV)

Make It POP! The power of prayer is incredible.

Prayer. How do we pray? Do our prayers go to God? How long should we pray? Give God time through prayer. Talk to Him. Listen to Him. Anytime. Anywhere. Pray how you feel led to pray. Keep it simple. It's just conversation. Yet the outcomes of such prayer are so powerful. As you pray, things in your life will change. The power of simple prayer will Make it Pop!

In my own life, the power of prayer has brought these results:

The cancer could no longer be found.

As the real estate sign was going up in the yard, a woman came by and said that she drove down from another town and was hoping to buy a house in that area that weekend. She happened to be a cash buyer.

In the last hours of his life, he opened his eyes, communicated with his wife and gave acknowledgement that he was ready to go to heaven. His family was amazed and so thankful.

In spite of being born 3 months early and only weighing 3 pounds, she was making it day by day.

Your thoughts…

BOLD

Be stouthearted
Out of comfort zone
Leaning on God's strength
Destined & Determined

"I think a hero is an ordinary individual who finds strength to persevere and endure in spite of overwhelming obstacles."

Christopher Reeve

Psalm 138:3
"In the day when I cried out, You answered me, And made me bold with strength in my soul." (NKJV)

When we become confident of who we are in Christ–we can walk forward in boldness. How exciting it is to know that God gives us this divine enablement, empowering us with spiritual power and authority. We are to come boldly into His presence and walk with authority.

Boldness is defined as cheerful courage, opposite of cowardice, frankness and candor. When boldness comes from the spirit it comes with a divine enablement that is graced.

Step out in boldness. Rely on Him. Look at all the situations you are involved in. Where could you take a bolder stand? Do the people around you know that you have a backbone for God? Do they expect you to stand firmly on those things that matter?

Stand strong. Be bold with God's strength.

Your thoughts…

UNITY

Unified Spirit
Necessary
In mind &
Thought by
You and others

"The reason why the world lacks unity, and lies broken and in heaps, is because man is disunited with himself."

Ralph Waldo Emerson (1803-1882)

Ephesians 4:1-6
"As a prisoner for the Lord, then I urge you to live a life worthy of the calling you have received. Be completely humble and gentle; be patient, bearing with one another in love. Make every effort to keep the unity of the Spirit—just as you were called to one hope when you were called, one Lord, one faith, one baptism, one God and Father of all who is over all and through all and in all." (NIV)

Why is there so much division between God's people? Why have we allowed our hearts and minds to become hardened or fixed on our opinions? Are we open to believe with a unified spirit?

As these questions swirled in my head, the story in Acts 10 became so clear. It began with God speaking to Cornelius, a Gentile, in a vision where an angel of God appeared and told him to send for Peter, a Jew. Interesting enough, at the same time, God was working on Peter. Peter had a vision where a great white sheet was bound at the 4 corners. In it were all kinds of 4-footed animals of the earth. A voice told Peter to kill and eat those animals. Peter told God that he couldn't because he had never eaten anything common or unclean. The voice spoke to him again and basically told him what God had cleansed, he must not call common. This was done 3 times and the objects he saw were taken up to heaven. While Peter was wondering what this was all about, Cornelius' men showed up at his door wanting to take him back to Cornelius' house.

Peter was open to the Spirit of God telling him to go with them, doubting nothing. (Acts 10:20) As Cornelius and Peter were brought under one roof, the two men came in unity. Peter opened his mouth and said,

"In truth I perceive that God shows no partiality. But in every nation whoever fears Him and works righteousness is accepted by Him." (Acts 10:34) Then the Spirit fell upon all of them together.

At that time, who would have thought that God would have put Gentiles and Jews under one roof? Without willing hearts and open minds, these men would not have experienced the unity that occurred.

Your thoughts…

PART VI

MEDITATE ON THESE PROMISES

Nuggets to notice

"The Lord showed me, so that I did not dwell in these temples which men had commanded and set up, but in people's hearts...His people were His temple, and He dwelt in them."

George Fox

ENOUGH

Everything
Needed is
Obtained
Unceasingly from
God's
Hand

"All of You is more than enough for all of me.

For every thirst and every need, you satisfy me with Your love.

All I have with you is more than enough."

Praise Music, Woodridge

Matthew 14:16-18
"But Jesus said to them, 'They do not need to go away. You give them something to eat.' And they said to Him, 'We have here only five loaves and two fish.' He said, 'Bring them here to me.' Then He commanded the multitudes to sit down on the grass. And He took the five loaves and the two fish, and looking up to Heaven, He blessed and broke and gave the loaves to the disciples; and the disciples gave to the multitudes." (NKJV)

MORE THAN ENOUGH
Can you imagine the disciples' anxiety as the crowd grew to 5,000 coming up the mountainside? How would they ever feed them? Phillip estimated 8 months wages would only provide each person 1 bite. Andrew quickly looked around utilizing resources, "Here is a boy with 5 small barley loaves and 2 fish." But he even felt that wouldn't go far among so many.

Here they were among their Savior who had performed many miraculous signs–Why would they even mutter of doubt or question? Immediately Jesus told the disciples to have the people sit down. In other words: Relax, recline–which puts them in a position to receive. And boy, did they!

As you read on to verses 20 and 21 it states; "So they all ate and were filled, and they took up 12 baskets full of the fragments that remained."

They had MORE THAN ENOUGH!

Your thoughts…

AHA

Always
Hearing
An answer

"Listen and be led."

L. M. Heroux

Proverbs 3:5-6
"Trust God from the bottom of your heart; don't try to figure out everything on your own. Listen for God's voice in everything you do, everywhere you go. He's the one who will keep you on track."
(The Message)

Do you need an "Aha" right now?

When we stop, listen, and look up–God answers. His answer may be a nudge, prompt or in "His still voice." All of a sudden what was not clear becomes clear. All of a sudden someone comes into the picture that is part of the solution.

God is always there with you. Ask Him to speak to you right now.

Samuel is a great example for us. Listening to God was his first divine experience! He thought Eli was calling him each time and finally Eli told him to go back to bed and answer God's call by saying, "Speak Lord, for your servant hears." (1 Samuel 3:10) (NKJV)

To begin knowing what God is trying to tell us, we have to get in a position to hear. You will begin to experience that God is always there, always speaking... but it is up to us to hear His answers.

Your thoughts…

POWER

Pursuit
Of God's
Wisdom
Equals
Righteousness

"Our scientific power has outrun our spiritual power. We have guided missiles and misguided men."

Martin Luther King Jr.

Isaiah 42:6
"I the Lord have called you in righteousness and will hold your hand; I will keep you and give you as a covenant to the people, a light to the Gentiles." (NKJV)

Power derives from 4 Hebrew words as shown below. As I studied each of these scriptures listed, I have written out an interpretation of the meaning of power that is used.

Koach–capability, ability (Deut. 8:18) Our ability to earn wealth comes from Him alone.
Exousia–authority, right to act (Mark 3:15) God gives us power to touch lives.
Kratos–effective, power shown in reigning (1 Tim 6:16) Speaks of the King of Kings that no one has seen.
Dunamis–might, great force (Acts 4:33) The disciples gave witness in a mighty way.

What a difference power takes on when it derives from God's power and not ours. His power is more than we can ever make happen. It is the power of the King of Kings and Lord of Lords.

Your thoughts…

MORE

Mindset
Of
Restoration w/o
Exceptions

"Prosperity is just around the corner."

Herbert Hoover

Ephesians 3:20
"Now to Him who is able to do exceedingly abundantly above all that we ask or think according to the power that works in us." (NKJV)

Why is it so challenging to think of exceptional outcomes with no limits?

Do we truly trust God to the fullest? Do we truly believe we are worthy to receive more than we can ask or think of?

So many times we limit God from doing more. We take over. Remember, the Spirit moves without limit. (John 3:34b) In this verse it states the following: "For the one whom God has sent speaks the Words of God, for He gives the Spirit without limit." This promise gives us confidence to trust the Spirit in an incredible way, for MORE!

Your thoughts...

PURPOSE

Plan
Ultimately
Reserved for each
Person
Obviously
Sent with
Eternal Intentions

"In a fabulous necklace I had to admire the anonymous string by which the whole thing was strung together."

Weavings Journal, Vol. 5 #5

Isaiah 14:24
"The Lord Almighty has sworn; 'Surely as I have planned so it will be, and as I have purposed so it will stand.'" (NIV)

A purpose is a deliberate plan, an intention, a design. Each one of us has a purpose in our life.

Recognize the gifts that are within you. Notice the moments when God is working through you with the gifts that he has given you. Through prayer and study you will become aware of your gifts and abilities that God has made in you. Maybe it is touching lives of the people in your neighborhood or at work.

What you will recognize is there will be passion around your gifting. The call becomes the dream that enters your consciousness. And you have a need to move in that direction. You create goals to help you get there. You will have such passion because it will consume you.

Your thoughts…

REVEAL

Revelation
Exposing God's
Vision & Purpose for you—
Expressing His
Absolute
Love for you

"Every revelation rightly understood and acted upon clears the way for a higher one."

Unknown

Amos 3:7
"Surely the Lord God does nothing unless He reveals His secret to His servants the prophets." (NKJV)

Over the last 5 years I have tried to grasp how much God loves me. In spite of the areas that I have failed in, I know he will help me through and teach me how to become more like Him.

I ask Him to reveal Himself to me. I ask Him to reveal what He wants me to do for Him.

It has not always been clear to me but through study and prayer, God has directed me in His path. I have learned that as I pray and seek Him, He gives me signs along the way. As I have stepped forward, feel peace about the step and decision made, I know as I go. Over a period of time, I have gained more insight about God's direction. He is always willing to reveal His plan to us.

Your thoughts…

VISION

Visual
Image from the
Spirit
In divine communication of
Oneself–
Necessary to fulfill God's purpose

"The visionary disciplines himself or herself to see the world always as if he or she had only just seen it for the first time."

Colin Wilson

Proverbs 29:18
"Where there is no vision, the people perish." (KJV)

God wants you to place all your trust in Him. He has a vision for your life. He has a purpose for your existence. How fulfilling it is when that is understood.

Look at yourself and reflect on what strengths you have. What is it about you that is born within you? What comes easy for you? Helping others? Encouraging those around you? Teaching? Leading? Getting the job done? Whatever it may be, begin to know these things. Notice the things you do well and when you do them, time flies. Focus on things that bring you fulfillment. Then, ask God to show you His vision for your life in using those qualities to make a difference in this world to honor Him.

You will be amazed how the clarity comes. God's vision will become your vision.

Your thoughts…

RIPE

Ready for the
Impossible to become
Possible
Everyday

"It often happens that I wake at night and begin to think about a serious problem and decide I must tell the Pope about it. Then I wake up completely and remember I am the Pope."

Pope John XXIII

Mark 10:27
"But Jesus looked at them and said, 'With men it is impossible, but not with God; for with God all things are possible.'" (NKJV)

How can we develop a continual mindset of "The time is ripe?"

How do we live expecting the unexpected? By utilizing the power of the Holy Spirit, we can see things become and change before our very eyes. Today let us look at every situation before us with new eyes. Let us expect the impossible to become possible in our family, with our friends, at our work, in our churches, schools and communities.

Your thoughts…

SIGN

Significant
Indication that
God is
Near

"What seems to be a great loss or punishment often turns out to be a blessing. I know, through my own experience, that God never closes one door without opening another."

Yolanda D. Herron

Psalm 86:7
"In the day of my trouble, I will call to you, for you will answer me." (NKJV)

This word came to me in the wee hours of the morning. I had prayed for specific direction and was holding on to scriptures where prophets were given clear signs. It is so powerful when we understand that God wants to reveal His plan to us. He wants us to see his prompts, feel His nudges and acknowledge His signs.

A sign is something that points to, or represents, something larger or more important than itself. In the Old Testament, most references point to the miracles produced by God to help deliver the Hebrew people from slavery in Egypt. (Exodus 7:3, Isaiah 8:18) In the New Testament the word "signs" is linked with both miracles and wonders. (Acts 2:22, 2 Corinthians 12:12, Hebrews 2:4) The word occurs frequently in the Gospel of John, pointing to the deeper, symbolic meaning of the miracles performed by Jesus. (Concordance NKJV)

Today I encourage you to pray for signs so you are giving God the opportunity to show you the next step and direction He wants you to go.

The signs are all around you.

Get ready to receive!

Your thoughts…

CALLED

Come
As the
Lord
Leads
Expecting
Direction

"None of us will ever accomplish anything excellent or commanding except when he listens to this whisper which is heard by him alone."

Ralph Waldo Emerson (1803-1882)

Isaiah 42:6
"I the Lord, have called you in righteousness, and will hold your hand; I will keep you and give you as a covenant to the people, as a light to the Gentiles." (NKJV)

I will never forget the day I was in a colleague's office during a break. I was expressing this strong pull on my life that I couldn't identify specifically. All I could tell her was that I felt a change coming and that God was laying a strong desire on my life to help others.

My friend took a book that was placed in the back of her bookcase. She opened, "Utmost For His Highest" and read the message for that specific day. That message was written for me! We read a powerful message about how God places a purposeful calling on each of our lives. When we recognize the call from Him–**the call becomes the need**.

I knew from that moment on God was calling me to respond. We sat in that tiny office with all the demands of our work around us yet only focused on the message we held. Acknowledging God's call on my life was transforming.

From that day on my focus became centered around God's purpose. His call for me to serve.

My friend, what is your call?

Your thoughts…

SILENCE

"We need to find God, and he cannot be found in noise and restlessness. God is the friend of silence. See how nature– trees, flowers, grass–grows in silence; see the stars, moon and the sun, how they grow in silence...we need silence to touch souls."

Mother Teresa

In silence I cry out to you
Hear my cry
For your hand to come down
From the heavens and
Touch my fingertips

In silence I cry out to you
Hear my cry
For your soul to touch my heart
Heal it
Strengthen it
Revive it

In silence I raise my hands
Hear my praise
For your promise is steadfast
Your word is my rock
Your love is insatiable
Your grace is unexplainable

In silence I come to you

Thoughts to ponder…..

What does it take to get us silent?
Silent before God.
Is it pain or concern?
Is it lack of handling a situation myself?

Or do I just sit silent before him, reverent, praising him?
Whatever the reason—
Silence before God allows Him to speak to you in a way like never before.
Silence empowers knowledge.

Your thoughts...

PART VII

A VALUED GIFT

Nuggets of gold

"Let God have you, and let God love you—and don't be surprised if your heart begins to hear music you've never heard and your feet learn to dance as never before."

Max Lucado

BLESSED

Believing &
Living–
Expecting the
Spirit of
Salvation to
Extend
Deliverance

"Incredible as it may seem, God wants our companionship. He wants to have us close to Him. He wants to be a father to us, to shield us, to protect us, to counsel us, and to guide us in our way through life."

Billy Graham

Matthew 5:3-11
"Blessed are the poor in spirit, For theirs is the kingdom of heaven.
Blessed are those who mourn, For they shall be comforted.
Blessed are the meek, For they shall inherit the earth.
Blessed are those who hunger and thirst for righteousness, For they shall be filled.
Blessed are the merciful, For they shall obtain mercy.
Blessed are the pure in heart, For they shall see God.
Blessed are the peacemakers, For they shall be called sons of God.
Blessed are those who are persecuted for righteousness' sake,
For theirs is the kingdom of heaven." (NKJV)

We are given specific direction of what qualities and characteristics God wants us to have and the blessing that will come. Whatever has happened in our lives or whatever we are going through right now...God extends His deliverance and His blessing.

Your thoughts…

HEAL

Having
Every
Affliction
Lifted

"Nothing...refreshes and aids a sick man so much as the affection of his friends."

Senaca The Younger
"On the Healing Power of the Mind"

Jeremiah 33:3
"Call to Me, and I will answer you, and show you great and mighty things, which you do not know." (NKJV)

Jeremiah 33:6
"Behold, I will bring it health and healing; I will heal them and reveal to them the abundance of peace and truth." (NKJV)

Malachi 4:2
"But to you who fear my name, The Sun of Righteousness shall arise with healing in His wings…" (NKJV)

God has the power to heal. As we look at His promises, we have every reason to trust and count on His healing. In His Word, we are given example after example of His ability to heal physically and emotionally.

At the same time, we see how healing in this world doesn't always come as we had hoped–which makes it hard to understand. It can make us doubt. But it is important to focus on applying faith to each situation that comes our way and walk forward asking for healing.

It is amazing to see God work in the midst of "needed" healing. Maybe the outcome we are hoping for is different than what we will experience, but in every case there is work that God accomplishes. Many times outcomes occur that we never dreamt of. Families come together, a life or relationship is changed forever, staff is touched, priorities get clarified or relationships are formed that weren't there before. Maybe work is accomplished that we never see, but it is done in a divine way. Whatever the outcome…we approach the situation with faith in God, that His will be done.

Never wavering from the hope of healing, amazing things will happen before us.

This Nugget is dedicated to Wayne and Elaine as they heal.

Your thoughts…

WISDOM

Wise
Insight from the
Spirit
Determining the
Opportunities for
Ministry

"Wisdom is the ability to look at all things from the point of view of God.

The invariable mark of wisdom is to see the miraculous in the common."

Ralph Waldo Emerson
(1803-1882)

Isaiah 11:2
"The Spirit of the Lord shall rest upon Him,
The Spirit of wisdom and understanding,
The Spirit of counsel and might,
The Spirit of knowledge and of the fear of the Lord." (NKJV)

In the book of James, he states that if any of us lack wisdom we are to ask God who gives to all liberally and without approach and it will be given to him. Right after those words we are reminded to ask him in faith with no doubting because, "He who doubts is like a wave of the sea driven and tossed by the wind." (James 1:6) (NKJV)

For years, I prayed for wisdom. I felt it was an area that I was lacking in. I had read about the Lord promising Solomon wisdom and how he granted it to him. I wanted wisdom too. I decided to read about how Solomon obtained wisdom and see if I could do the same.

In 1 Kings 4:29-30 it states:
"And God gave Solomon wisdom and exceedingly great understanding, and largeness of heart like the sand on the seashore. His wisdom excelled the wisdom of all the men of the East and all the wisdom of Egypt." (NKJV)

I didn't need that much, but I wanted to ask like Solomon did and in receiving this gift of wisdom, I would have insight into God's direction for my life and increased knowing. How comforting it is to know that we have access to such a beautiful gift of practical wisdom and precious insight.

And, all we have to do is spend uninterrupted time alone with God seeking His Word.

The rest will come.

Your thoughts...

COURAGE

Confidence to
Overcome–
Utilizing God's
Resources
And faith in His
Grace that is
Exceptional

"Courage is what it takes to stand up and speak. Courage is also what it takes to sit down and listen."

Winston Churchill

"Courage is contagious. When a brave man takes a stand, the spines of others are often stiffened."

Billy Graham

Deuteronomy 31:6
"Be strong and of good courage, do not fear or be afraid of them; for the Lord your God, He is the one who goes with you. He will not leave you or forsake you." (NKJV)

What a comforting promise we have to depend on! Basically, God is telling us that no matter what comes our way, we are not to worry because He will be there with us. He will never leave us or let us down.

Joshua is a life example of the need for courage. He was taking a risk for God and needed courage to handle the situation he was given. He was assigned the task of getting a slew of Israelites across the Jordan River. The whole reason was so they could claim the Land of Promise. It is written that God reminded Joshua by telling him 3 times to have courage. Really the only thing we have to overcome is fear or discouragement creeping in. One way we can do this is to stay close to the Lord and don't allow for negatives to enter in. Pray for protection.

To sum it up, two quotes come to mind:
"Courage is a special kind of knowledge: the knowledge of how to fear what ought to be feared and how not to fear what ought not to be feared."

David Ben-Gurion

*"Success is never final.
Failure is never fatal.
Courage is what counts."*

Sir Winston Churchill

Your thoughts...

MIRACLE

Mirror my ways
Instill my words in your heart
Rely on me alone
Acknowledge my power
Commit your life to me
Live with Hope
Expect the unexpected

"Where there is great love there are always miracles."

Willa Cather (1876-1947)

John 14:11
"Believe me when I say that I am the father and the father is in me; or at least believe on the evidence of the miracles themselves." (NIV)

God wants to do miracles in our life. He has given His Word to show us many miracles that He made possible.

Acts 4:13-16
"Now when they saw the boldness of Peter and John, and perceived that they were uneducated and untrained men, they marveled. And they realized that they had been with Jesus. And seeing the man who had been healed standing with them, they could say nothing against it. But when they had commanded them to go aside out of the council, they conferred among themselves saying, 'What shall we do to these men? For indeed, that a notable miracle has been done through them is evident to all who dwelt in Jerusalem, and we cannot deny it.'" (NKJV)

How can we live expecting the unexpected in this time of the world? He is still God of the universe. What miracle do you need right now? How can you get in a place to believe and receive the miracles that God has waiting for you?

It is important to have a mindset of miracles. Always believing, always expecting.

Your thoughts…

FAVOR

Father's faithfulness
Advances you
Virtually with
Outstanding
Results

"Favor from God is the greatest compliment we can ever receive. It is like God having our picture in his billfold and on His refrigerator; gleaming when He looks down."

D. Kilgore

Luke 1:28
"And having come in, the angel said to her, 'Rejoice, highly favored one, the Lord is with you, blessed are you among women.' " (NKJV)

Favor derives from the greek word, **Ratson** *(rah-tzoon)*; Strong #7522. It refers especially to what is pleasing and desirable to God. (NKJV)

The favor of God is a wonderful thing. With favor, He will bring you through with a divine outcome. It will be unexplainable in the world's eye.

I have a friend that always responds to me with the same response when I share an amazing something that God has done. She always remarks that she isn't surprised as she knows I have a direct connection to God. I always reply that we ALL have the same direct connection, we just have to plug it in.

I think what we are both really talking about is God's favor. It is powerful. What an incredible thing to have accomplished in finding favor with God.

We are reminded in Hebrews 6:11-12 that we are to:
"Show the same diligence to the full assurance of hope until the end, that you do not become sluggish, but imitate those whose faith and patience inherit the promises."

Your thoughts…

SUDDENLY

Spirit
Ultimately
Delivers even in
Difficult circumstances—
Explanations
Not needed

"The breeze of God's grace is blowing continually. You have to set your sail to catch that breeze."

*Swami Prabhavananda
(1893-1976)*

It's a Suddenly!

2 Chronicles 29:36
"Then Hezekiah and all the people rejoiced that God had prepared the people, since the events took place so **suddenly**." (NKJV)

Malachi 3:1
"'Behold I send my messenger, and he will prepare the way before Me. And the Lord, whom you seek, will **suddenly** come to His temple, even the Messenger of the covenant, in whom you delight. Behold, He is coming.' Says the Lord of Hosts." (NKJV)

Luke 2:13-14
"And **suddenly** there was with the angel a multitude of the heavenly host praising God and saying: 'Glory to God in the highest, And on earth peace, goodwill toward men!'" (NKJV)

I love **SUDDENLYS!** I pray for them quite often. Even though I know it is in His timing and His will… I pray expecting **SUDDENLYS** and hope God wills it to be.

I pray…
Suddenly God's plan will be revealed.
Suddenly the help will come.
Suddenly my friend will experience peace in the midst of pain.
Suddenly a solution will become evident.

Suddenly a heart will become softened.
Suddenly the Buccaneers will score a touchdown. Come on Stovall!!

(I am just joking on the last one! Well, I did do that one game but we don't need to go there, do we?)

Do you need a suddenly? Do you have faith for a suddenly?

Your thoughts…

JOY

Jubilant Spirit
Overflows in
You

"As we grow in our capacities to see, and enjoy the joys that God has placed in our lives, life becomes a glorious experience of discovering His endless wonders."

Unknown

John 15:11
"I have told you this so that my joy may be in you and that your joy may be complete." (NIV)

Joy comes in the journey. Remember, joy is always out there ahead of us. In spite of how we are feeling at the moment, what trial is at our feet, what may have happened that we never expected; we can strive to have joy. The more we seek God in every situation, be it fortunate or not fortunate, our efforts will bring joy.

1) Joy supersedes circumstances. It is a gift you receive so humbly– receive it!
2) Joy is rock solid. It is an overall sense of well-being so you don't need to crave pleasure and happiness.
3) Joy is within you, so cultivate your inner life.

Your thoughts…

LAUGH

Live it up
And
Unwind with
God's
Help

"'Live to Love' was my father's motto. 'Live to Laugh' is mine."

Hannah Cowley

"Laughter is the Music of the Soul"

Unknown

Job 18:21
"He will fill our mouth with laughing–and your lips with rejoicing." (NKJV)

Let's laugh together today....

"If a man watches 3 football games in a row–he should be declared legally dead."
Erma Bombeck

"Man has his will–but woman has her way."
Oliver Wendall Holmes

"Never eat more than you can lift."
Miss Piggy

"Leisure time is when your wife can't find you."
Unknown

"God is everywhere.....except on the golf course."
Billy Graham

"I stopped believing in Santa Claus when I was six. Mother took me to see him in a department store and he asked me for my autograph."
Shirley Temple Black

"I'm sick of following my dreams. I'm just going to ask them where they're going and hook up with them later."
Mitch Hedberg
(1968-2005)

Your thoughts…

AMAZING

Astounding
Miracles with
Absolute
Zeal–
Involving
No other than
God

"May your trails be crooked, winding, lonesome, dangerous, leading to the most amazing view. May your mountains rise into and above the clouds."

Edward Abbey

Ephesians 3:20
"Now to Him who is able to do exceedingly abundantly above all that we ask or think, according to the power that works in us." (NKJV)

Amazing….Amazing….Amazing! When have you used this word? It represents one being astounded and taken back. Often it relates to events that are unexplainable.

God wants to surprise us….in amazing ways!

Your thoughts…

CELEBRATE

Christ's
Everlasting
Love
Evolves
Brilliantly–
Radiating
Absolute
Thankfulness
Everyday

"Celebrate what you want to see more of."

Thomas J. Peters

Deuteronomy 16:15b
"For the Lord your God will bless you in all your harvest and in all the work of your hands, and your joy will be complete." (NIV)

Celebrate and embrace the freedom that God gives you today, this month, this season, this year. You have a new identity when you are a child of Christ. You are no longer a slave to this world. Seek the freedom that Christ offers you through your faith.

Celebrate all that God gives you. Celebrate by praising Him everyday. Celebrate by learning more about Him. Celebrate by practicing "His ways" in all we do–

Honoring God by faith.

"Stop worrying about the potholes in the road and celebrate the journey."

Barbara Hoffman

Your thoughts…

"The most beautiful stones have been tossed by the wind and washed by the waters and polished to brilliance by life's strongest storms."

Unknown